To ▮▮▮ & ▮▮▮ —

May you Recieve a blessing from Reading my Story!

I love you both

▮▮▮▮▮▮
(▮▮▮▮)

The Devil Made Them Do it at Tiny Town Church

Sophie Baker

WESTBOW PRESS®
A DIVISION OF THOMAS NELSON
& ZONDERVAN

Copyright © 2015 Sophie Baker.

All rights reserved. No part of this book may be used or reproduced by any means, graphic, electronic, or mechanical, including photocopying, recording, taping or by any information storage retrieval system without the written permission of the publisher except in the case of brief quotations embodied in critical articles and reviews.

Cover design and chalk drawing, *"The Devil at Tiny Town Church"*, was created and drawn by the author's husband, with written statement of ownership transferred to the author.

WestBow Press books may be ordered through booksellers or by contacting:

WestBow Press
A Division of Thomas Nelson & Zondervan
1663 Liberty Drive
Bloomington, IN 47403
www.westbowpress.com
1 (866) 928-1240

Because of the dynamic nature of the Internet, any web addresses or links contained in this book may have changed since publication and may no longer be valid. The views expressed in this work are solely those of the author and do not necessarily reflect the views of the publisher, and the publisher hereby disclaims any responsibility for them.

Any people depicted in stock imagery provided by Thinkstock are models, and such images are being used for illustrative purposes only.
Certain stock imagery © Thinkstock.

ISBN: 978-1-5127-0658-1 (sc)
ISBN: 978-1-5127-0660-4 (hc)
ISBN: 978-1-5127-0659-8 (e)

Library of Congress Control Number: 2015912592

Print information available on the last page.

WestBow Press rev. date: 08/03/2015

Contents

Dedication ix
Preface xiii

The Foundation

Chapter 1　　My Story 3
Chapter 2　　Ministry 101 14
Chapter 3　　Ministry as Calling 23
Chapter 4　　Satan's Seven plus Two 41

The Desert

Chapter 5　　The Devil in Sheep's Clothing 65
Chapter 6　　Politics in the Church? 84
Chapter 7　　Making Sense of it All 94
Chapter 8　　Holding the Church Hostage 98
Chapter 9　　Trouble in the Church 107

Healing and Moving Forward

Chapter 10　　We'll Just Call You Sister 129
Chapter 11　　Living in the Spirit 143

Chapter 12	Walking in the Light	156
Chapter 13	Abiding in Christ	161
Chapter 14	God's Time	172

"My task, which I am trying to achieve, is, by the power of the written word, to make you hear, to make you feel--it is, before all, to make you see."
Joseph Conrad, *Lord Jim*[1]

---

[1] Conrad, Joseph, *Lord Jim*; WWW.Goodreads.com. "Quotes about Writing".

Dedication

To "Alyce", who taught me how to forgive and not to judge others, especially according to my own perception; for perception is not the truth; it is merely that person's own view. Actual truth comes from God, and God alone knows the depths of our hearts! May God speak to your heart and enable you to see His gifts and goodness within each person you lead. May you be filled with His Spirit...

To all of our friends who supported me and my ministry at Tiny Town Church (you know who you are): I pray God's blessings upon each of you as we continue to journey together with our Lord...

To all our friends at "The Bible Church": your prayers sustained us, and your love, support and friendship gave us new hope. You are forever in our hearts...

To our new missionary friends, we praise God for your friendship, strength and faith that kept us looking upward and praising God for the blessings that were to come...

Always, to my dear tumbling coach, my mentor throughout my life: you have taught me how to live, love, be strong, and never quit. I love you...

To Mom and my brother who endured the pain of Tiny Town with me; your strength and love are amazing! I love you both...

To all of our amazing children: our lives have been quite an adventure and you continue to inspire me. I praise God for each of you and the blessings of spouses, grandchildren and great-grandchildren that God so graciously has given to us all…

To our 2nd daughter, the greatest Literary Guide on the planet: you are such an inspiration to me.

To the love of my life: you endured the pain of Tiny Town Church with me and God gave you the strength and understanding to help me see the blessings waiting on the other side of it all…

The above names, places and church names have been changed, or omitted, to prevent direct connection to, and/or identification of those involved.

In loving memory of Mom

May 19, 2015

Preface

"Watch out for false prophets. They come to you in sheep's clothing, but inwardly they are ferocious wolves. By their fruit you will recognize them… (Matthew 7:15-16; NIV[2])

This is a true story. I know that it is hard to believe that evil can appear in the most sacred of all places…our places of worship! But it does. I am thankful to Rebecca Nichols Alonzo who wrote about her parent's experiences in ministry in **The Devil in Pew Number Seven**[3]. God placed Rebecca's book before me just after the termination of my ministry at Tiny Town Church, and it confirmed to me that the harder God's people work and succeed for the Kingdom, the harder the devil is going to try to destroy it. I praise God for Rebecca and for her story.

This book was written to share with you what happened to me in one of my church appointments as a minister in one of the leading denominations; how evil attempted to destroy the ministry of a church and its pastor, and how God delivered

---

[2] Scripture quotations marked NIV are taken from the Holy Bible, *The NIV Rainbow Study Bible,* copyright © 2007 by Standard Publishing. Used by permission of Standard Publishing. All rights reserved. www.rainbowstudies.com; www.standardpub.com.

[3] Alonzo, Rebecca Nichols. **The Devil in Pew Number Seven.** 2012. Tyndale House Publishers, Inc. Tyndale Momentum. www.tyndalemomentum.com

this hurting and devastated pastor to a new ministry waiting in another land. This story is revealed, not out of anger, but out of love for our Lord and Savior, Jesus Christ and His church. I write this book using a pen name in order to protect my ministry, my friends and family, and all of those involved in the writing and publishing of this book. All names have been changed, all cities and states have been eliminated and all church and school names have been either changed or eliminated. Hopefully, through this story, all of God's people will become more involved in the ministry of the local church and changes can be made to rid our worship centers of the devil who may be sitting next to you!

This is not a Methodist problem. This is a problem that knows no denominational boundaries. For where the Holy Spirit is alive in the people of God, there will be evil trying to destroy their good fruits. In Tiny Town Church, the Holy Spirit was alive and moving among us. The church was experiencing new growth and excitement after a long series of negative events. The more active the Holy Spirit was, the more forceful the devil became in trying to destroy the ministry of the church and pastor as well as those who worshipped there.

Tiny Town Church, located in Small Town, America, is not the correct name. The names of the church, the town and state have been changed. The names of the main characters that are mentioned have also been changed to protect privacy as well as to enable healing of the church and congregation as they attempt to rebuild their lives. Where this happened and who was involved is not important. What is important is that it did happen; and it could happen to you, too!

Many times throughout this story, I speak of myself in the third person, "the pastor", so that the focus will stay on the situation and not on me personally. What happened to me at Tiny Town is happening to clergy and congregations throughout this country. Many church systems are structured in such a way that it encourages corporate philosophies and power struggles which lead to the "rising star" syndrome that equates to worldly, prideful, ungodly behaviors.

Please join me in prayer for all of our small membership churches and fellowships. The devil is most active in these areas of ministry because of the smaller numbers of worshipers and the availability to take control. I am convinced that there is power in numbers: the larger the body of believers, the more work the devil has to do, and the harder it is for him to achieve his goals.

I begin this journey with "My Story" because I think it is important for you, the reader, to know who I am and how I ended up in ministry. We then progress from there to "Church 101", a brief history of the organization of the Methodist Church since my story takes place in that ministry setting. And, because of this, I think it is important to lay a good foundation at the start. After all, it was a breakdown of this fundamental foundational base that led to the problems at Tiny Town Church.

More foundational information is presented in Chapter 3 with "Ministry as Calling": what is a minister, how do we get from here to there, and how does this relate to the problems at Tiny Town? Once these questions are answered, we are ready to dive into the story of Tiny Town Church with "Satan's Seven plus Two". Once you have the whole story, we will progress into the last third of the book: what the problem is and how do we fix it, and how did this pastor end up at "The Promised Land"; that "Land Beyond the River"; that "Land Flowing with Milk and Honey"! I'm not talking about "heaven"…I'm talking about that beautiful new life and ministry that our gracious God has given to us!

Grace and Peace to each of you as you read the Word, live the Faith, and love the Lord!

The Foundation

"Nevertheless, God's solid foundation stands firm, sealed with this inscription: 'The Lord knows those who are his, and 'Everyone who confesses the name of the Lord must turn away from wickedness'" (2 Timothy 2: 19, NIV).

1

My Story

"You did not choose me, but I chose you and appointed you to go and bear fruit—fruit that will last. Then the Father will give you whatever you ask in my name" (John 15: 16, NIV).

I start "My Story" with a brief family history to show our family's dedication to and involvement in Methodism from its very beginning in this country. All family names have been changed but the story and facts have not. After the family history, the foundation for the Tiny Town story starts to unfold!

Around 1680, Captain "1", a Merchant Mariner, made his way across the Atlantic again for his last voyage as a single man. Traveling on that ship was "Elaina" who would later become his bride after they arrived in America. Several years later, they married and had several children. One of their children, Captain "2" became the heir of our family lines on our father's side.

Captain 2 was born in 1686 and followed his father in the shipping business, later to become a ship's captain. According to stories told from our great-grandmother and a handwritten family history by her sister-in-law, Captain 1 and Captain 2 were merchant mariners who made many trips back and forth across the Atlantic bringing people and goods to the colonies. In England, Captain 1 was a member of the Church of England as was all of his family before him.

Captain 2 had three wives and twelve children. As the story goes from Great-Grandmother, the grandson of Captain 2, we'll call him "James", was a Lieutenant in the Minute Men and became an Anglican Priest in the mid 1700's. In 1779, he joined the "Methodist Society", and in 1781, he built a chapel on his plantation. The chapel James built was one of the first Methodist Meeting Houses in that territory for the Methodist Society. In December of 1784, the American Methodist preachers gathered at Baltimore and adopted the "Sunday Service" and the "Articles of Religion" as part of their actions in forming the new "Methodist Episcopal Church". It is exciting to know that, according to our grandmother's stories, James was in attendance there.

In 1799, James moved westward, and the little meeting house he left behind continued to have regular religious meetings. In 1801, he bought five-hundred acres in his new community and later built a log home there. Upon its completion in 1803, he moved his family there; and, together they built a large log barn on his land.

From 1803 to 1818, there were services of the early Methodist Episcopal Church held in that log barn. The first pastor there gathered the settlers of the new country into this very primitive sanctuary to hear the preaching of God's Word. In the weeks, months, and years ahead, that log barn echoed to the amazing preaching of such men as Bishops Francis Asbury, Whatcoat, McKendry, George and Lorenzo Dow, and the father and son,

Finley duo. In 1818 a church was built next to the site of the old log barn. The first religious organization of the township was declared on Christmas, 1802, with James and his wife and five former slaves as members of the class. After that date, there was an annual camp meeting held on the farm for thirty-four years. The result of this continued movement was the development of a stronghold of Methodism within that neighborhood. A beautiful brick building was erected in 1871, on the site of the old church.

Later, James donated this section of his land to the Methodist Church. While this building has been renovated several times, it is still an active Methodist Church and our relatives from James's family are buried there in the church's cemetery.

Our family continued to grow and become established there until our great-grandmother, "Mary" and her husband, "Jacob", grandson and nephew of James and his wife, moved south to the coast with their young family. There they quickly established themselves in the Methodist church. Their daughter and my grandmother, "Angela", would grow up and marry a handsome gentleman named "Noah", and they would have three sons. My father was their youngest.

Needless to say, my brother and I were born into the Methodist Church. Actually, we were born into the very church that our great grandparents, along with other young couples many years earlier, had formed and chartered. My father was so proud to say that he and his life-long friend were the first babies on the cradle role of that church. Our family church was the only church we knew until we grew up and went away to college, and it remains our home church to this day. We will always remember our spiritual formation that began there at our birth.

My brother answered the call into ministry just before he graduated from high school, and when he graduated, he went off to college and seminary. During our childhood, my brother and I spent every summer possible at our church camp. It was at this camp one summer when I accepted Jesus into my life. While we were raised in a Christian home with Christian parents, Jesus became my Lord and Savior that day at camp and I knew I would grow up to serve Him. That was God's first call on my life: to follow in His footsteps.

While I did not understand about "calling" at that early time in my life, I knew my life was changing. From that time on I would receive many calls from God for a change in direction according to His plan for my life. His second call on my life came when I was 21 years old. I was young and unsure exactly what a call was and how one was to feel when it came, but I knew that God needed me to help the sick, so I became a registered nurse.

God works in mysterious ways. I was working as an RN in the Intensive Care Unit of a local hospital. My youngest child was in the third grade and the rest of the children were grown and on their own. I visited friends who were nestled high in the mountains who were selling their dairy farm. While visiting there, I felt a tug on my heart to be there…to live there. There is no doubt in my mind that God called me there and to that dairy farm. So, my little girl and I left everything we knew and moved to the dairy farm; and together, we learned how to milk and care for our cows! Most of my preaching experience came from my first congregation of cows!

In the field of nursing, I ministered spiritually and medically to many types of sick and needy patients. I was saddened to leave my profession but was forced to make that decision when I fell down a flight of stairs and sustained injuries so severe that it prevented me from working as a nurse for many years. Living on a farm at the time, I was able to devote the next five years to healing, rehab, dairy farming, and breeding and raising dairy cattle. I began studying agriculture at the local university to obtain a degree in animal science in the hopes of going on to veterinary school upon graduation.

It was during these years that I started a Christian outreach program for our community. I began this program to help feed the needy in our church and community. I donated cattle yearly for butcher for those who applied for our program. Through this outreach program, many people were fed and many lives were changed. I cannot begin to explain the feeling that comes over a person when they deliver a freezer and a side of beef to a family who hasn't eaten meat in many months. There were many times that we left the homes in tears because of the blessings received through this gift. God truly blessed us through this ministry as I'm sure He did all of those who participated in this program.

Just after I started my last semester of undergraduate work, God called me into servant ministry. I felt inadequate and unprepared. Up to this time, my service for God had been on my terms and limited to a one-on-one experience through my nursing or in a group like choir or group activities that I supported but did not lead. I was extremely introverted and the thought of being up in front of a group as a leader, made me extremely nervous. So, while I knew that God wanted me in some form of ministry, I knew that He had a lot of work to do with me yet. After much prayer, I knew that I was being called to seminary; not so much to study for the ministry, but just to study and mature and grow in faith. I needed to immerse myself in the Word and to be matured so much that I could at least speak out loud in a group about what God was doing in my life.

I made several trips to the seminary prior to my graduation from undergraduate, and shortly before graduation I received an acceptance letter from them. A month or so later, I graduated from my undergraduate program with a BS degree in Animal Science. Two months later, I married my long-time friend and soul mate and together we began studies in seminary (see what happens when you listen to God!). When asked what my major was going to be, the only thing I could think of was Christian Education. After all, that's what all women in ministry became when I was growing up in the sixties. I never even heard of a woman preacher until much later in my life. So, Christian Education was to be my major!

During our first chapel service at seminary, my call into servant ministry was more clearly defined to me and I knew immediately that God was calling me into the pastoral ministry. It hit me like a ton of bricks. I could not believe it. I am the person who could not get up in front of a group and speak unless they were nurses, or unless I was tumbling across the stage performing my much loved acrobatics. How could I do this? But, I was sure of this call and I knew that God had placed upon my heart the passion for pastoral ministry.

Not long after I started seminary my husband had open heart surgery very unexpectedly. A few months after his recovery, my Dad died. As our family tried to put the pieces of our lives back together again, Mom decided she wanted to move to her home town in another state to be close to her remaining brothers. Since this was a family group decision, we all prayed about this and felt that this would be a good opportunity for our mother to be with her three brothers in their later years. So we sold the farm and we moved.

We moved back to the small town of my mother's birth. In fact, we bought a house that was built on the very property where my maternal grandparents had homesteaded upon their immigration in the very early 1900's. Soon after our arrival, we became active members of our family Methodist Church, and we immediately felt right at home.

The pastor—"Larry"— of our church took a special interest in me at first because I was in seminary and studying for the ministry. So he gave me a lot of church responsibilities, which would be very helpful later when I had a church of my own. It was at this time and under Larry's supervision that I entered the candidacy program for ordained ministry.

We began singing in the church services and events. Up to this time I only sang in the choir. But, our pastor knew I was studying for the ministry and, so far, had not been up in front of a group at all; I think he was determined to help me overcome this stage fright I had. So we began singing, and every Sunday, we sang. The congregation loved the guitar music and they said they loved our singing—I think they were just being nice. But, we sang, and sang, and sang.

What that did was this: it put a song in my heart and a message in my soul. The stage fright was gone and I was on my way into Ministry. Not long after that, I received my first appointment at a small rural church as a student pastor. I remained there even after

I graduated from seminary and had a wonderful ministry there for many years. God's love and grace flowed among the saints there and there was no doubt that our ministry was blessed.

I became a certified candidate for ordained ministry while serving as a student pastor and the next year, graduated from seminary with the Master of Divinity degree. Realizing the need for additional leadership and worship classes, I began working on and completed the studies for the Master of Arts in Christian Leadership degree. Upon completion of these studies and degrees, I thought I was prepared for ministry. I soon found out that I was not; and so I continued on with my studies which eventually led to a Doctor of Ministry degree in Pastoral Leadership.

I had encountered several bumps on the road to ministry. Very early I realized that women do not move through the maze of hurdles as fast as men do, especially young men right out of college and seminary. I started this process with two strikes against me: I was an older woman and I was also a second vocation pastor. I might add that my supervising experience as an RN for thirty years came into play too, as I was a perfectionist, a by the book person, and just a bit bossy. I knew these were areas I needed to work on too, but I never really thought that the men in ministry that I would come in contact with would be so bothered by these qualities; so much so that many would display ungodly behaviors toward me. This, I guess, was the biggest shock to me.

Larry, our home church pastor, was my awakener. He became irritated with me primarily when I would not let my young teenage son travel out of town to a ball game with him. He crossed boundaries with my son when he tried to convince him to go out of town with him, and became angry with us when we would not allow him to take our son with him. He tried on several occasions to sway his friends on the local ministry committee against me by telling them things about me that simply were not true. After many other strange events were noticed, the leadership group at our church decided to talk to him about this. He cursed at us and stormed out of the church and never came back. His behaviors for months leading up to this time were odd to say the least. Being a nurse, I immediately thought he had dementia or something. We all complained to his supervising clergy ("Billy"), but to no avail because Billy and Larry were personal friends. We tried to bring it to his attention that someone needed to talk to Larry because we all felt that this change in behavior was severe enough to warrant intervention of some sort. All of the complaints and pleas for help for our pastor and our church fell on deaf ears.

The sad thing about the Pastor Larry story is this. Larry was elderly and it is not unusual for someone of his age to have dementia or other disorders that cause a change in behaviors. Yet, because the leadership team of the church, composed of about seven to eight members including my husband and me, confronted him about his behavior, and because I was a ministry student, I got blamed for causing trouble for him and I was labeled a "troublemaker" by the ministry committee. This committee was made up of all of Larry's old time friends in ministry and they supported him. I was new to this process, a student, and a woman and it seemed that nothing was in my favor.

I was questioned about this incident at my next meeting with the committee. I questioned them as to why we, who are entering the ministry process, have to undergo a battery of psychological testing and an evaluation by a psychologist before we are granted our ministry license, yet the older ministers, and the ones who entered the ministry before this ruling became a requirement for ministry, the prime candidates for age related psych problems, never have to be evaluated! These issues were never addressed.

I thought this subject was put to rest. However, one member spoke up and said that I was "building quite a negative file" for myself with their committee, which caught me a bit off guard. I guess he didn't like what I had said. In all of this, I could not figure out what I had done that was so bad. Was it for loving my church so much that I wanted my pastor to be all that he was supposed to be as God's representative to the adults and children in our church? Could it have been for understanding that pastors are not exempt from medical and psychological problems, especially the elderly? Or maybe it was for understanding that all pastors are supposed to be held accountable for their actions?

Guess where Larry is today some six years after this incident? He is waiting to go to trial for several severe felony charges. This is the pastor we tried to get help for six years earlier. This was my mentor in ministry—God's servant sent to dwell among us and serve and lead. Many of our denominations are experiencing these same sorts of things that simply get pushed aside and overlooked.

This was my introduction to the ministry of the church and the politics that surround us. I had never thought there were politics involved in ministry. I had not learned about this in seminary. I had never encountered this during my many years as a church member and worker before going into seminary. And, I had not encountered this during the years of my brother's ministry previous to mine. Yet I would soon find that this was only an introduction to how our ministry is just like other corporations in the fight up the corporate ladder. And, out of it all, I would come to realize that these problems occur primarily in the small membership churches across our country.

It was at this time that God called me to become ordained non-denominationally. I could justify becoming a licensed pastor within the denomination, as this gave me a platform to preach and teach God's Word; but I just could not give in to the politics that had consumed the church that I loved so much.

2

Ministry 101

"The Spirit of the Sovereign Lord is on me, because the Lord has anointed me to preach good news to the poor. He has sent me to bind up the brokenhearted, to proclaim freedom for the captives and release from darkness for the prisoners...to comfort all who mourn, and provide for those who grieve..."(Isaiah 61: 1, 2, 3; NIV).

I don't think we can go further until I give a brief overview about the organization of the Methodist Church since my experience occurred there. I would like to also point out here that I am still on the membership role of our local Methodist Church. My foundation and education is Biblical and Methodist. I have a deep love for my spiritual up-bringing and a deep appreciation for my roots as a Methodist. However, these problems can occur in any church anywhere and are most frequently seen in the small membership church.

Like any big organization, the Methodist church is divided into smaller groups for easy management, has an administrative order of governing and it has a structure similar to the United States government. The legislative branch is the General Conference and the Supreme Court is the Judicial Council.

Bishops would be comparable to the Office of the President, but the Methodist Church has no single general officer or executive. The Council of Bishops is the highest governing authority and they elect a president who serves for two years. He or she presides over the Council of Bishops as outlined in the Constitution of the UMC and the **Book of Discipline of the United Methodist Church**[4]. The Council of Bishops is made up of all of the bishops of the UMC including all of those who are retired. This group is supposed to provide leadership for the entire United Methodist Church. In addition, the Council of Bishops presides over the General Conference of the UMC which is held every four years and to which all of the churches in the UM system elect delegates, both lay and clergy, for representation[5].

The first division of the church is into *Jurisdictions*. In the United States of America, The United Methodist Church is divided into five jurisdictions: Northeastern, Southeastern, North Central, South Central and Western. These provide some program and leadership training events to support the annual conferences. Every four years the jurisdictional conferences meet to elect new bishops and select members of general boards and agencies. The United Methodist Churches located outside the United States are

---

[4] The United Methodist Church; Secretary of the General Conference and Committee on Correlation and Editorial Revision; **The Book of Discipline of the United Methodist Church;** The United Methodist Publishing House: Nashville, TN. Refer to this footnote for each future entry of the **Book of Discipline** and/or **The Book of Discipline of the United Methodist Church or UMC**.

[5] Tuell, Jack M. **The Structure of the United Methodist Church.** 2005-2008 Edition. Abingdon Press: Nashville, TN. Page 129.

organized into central conferences, much like the jurisdictions we have in the United States. There are seven central conferences: Africa, Central and Southern Europe, Congo, Germany, Northern Europe, Philippines, and West Africa.

The Jurisdictions are divided into Annual Conferences. The annual (sometimes referred to as 'regional') conference is described by the church's **Book of Discipline** as the "basic unit" of the church. An annual conference may cover an entire state, only part of the state, or even parts of two or more states. There are also three missionary conferences in the United States, which rely upon the denomination as a whole for funding. The United States has sixty-three annual conferences, supervised by fifty bishops. There are fifty-nine annual conferences in Africa, Europe, and the Philippines, which are supervised by eighteen bishops. Each annual conference has as its head, or supervisor, one bishop. Each year—usually in May, June, or July—all clergy members and an equal number of lay members selected from the local churches attend their conference's annual conference session and meet together to worship, fellowship, and conduct the business of the conference. This gathering may last three to five days. During these sessions, members of the conference hear reports of past and ongoing work; adopt future goals, programs and budgets; ordain clergy members as deacons and elders; and elect delegates to jurisdictional and general conferences (every four years). The bishop of that particular conference presides over these meetings[6].

The conferences are further divided into districts, each with a supervising clergy known as a District Superintendent. There

---

[6] www.umc.org; *The Structure of the United Methodist Church*; official website for the United Methodist Church.

are many districts in each conference. Every supervising clergy from the districts form the bishop's cabinet, are supervised by their bishop, and each of these supervising clergy supervise the group of individual clergy in their respective districts. Each of these clergy are pastors of the local churches in that district. So, the supervising chain of command, so to speak, is bishop to DS (Supervising Clergy or SC); local church pastor to local church.

Specifically, what do the supervising clergy, the district superintendents do? According to Tuell[7], one of the duties of a DS is to be a pastor to the pastors and their families in his or her district. In addition, the DS is an authority figure for the pastors he supervises but it is clear that he or she has no authority to tell a local pastor what to do. The pastor is the pastor in charge and responsible for what happens in his/her church. The DS also has no authority to tell the laity of the church what to do. The laity of the local church are governed in their actions by the policy of the charge conference of their church and of their pastor. Actually, the true authority of the DS is more indirect than direct and is revealed in two areas: seeing that the provisions of the ***Book of Discipline of the United Methodist Church*** are observed and in the appointive process for the pastors and churches in their district. The ***Book of Discipline*** is considered to be the rule book of the church; the employment contract of the church; the book of law for the church. As pastors, we are to lead our congregations according to the rules outlined in this book. At the same time, those who supervise the pastors are supposed to follow the rules, laws and guidelines in this book in their supervision and provide

---

[7] Tuell, Jack M. ibid.

support for their pastors as an official resource and interpreter of these rules, laws and guidelines.

While we all certainly hope and pray that each bishop, DS, and pastor would follow the rules outlined in the **Book of Discipline**, they each are human and, because of this, are subject to human motives, desires, agendas and sin. This is information that one never learns in seminary. The farther into ministry I progressed, the more I felt like I was in the middle of a big business, fighting my way up the corporate ladder. I began to feel strangled by the man-made and unholy rules I encountered and actions of some of my colleagues.

I began seminary with all of the initial courses required of all students. I was blessed that my husband could attend my classes on campus with me. Our time together with our class and professors was amazing and life changing. Especially amazing was worship in our chapel on campus. I will never forget my first experience in chapel worship: God spoke to me and called me into pastoral ministry. I knew this without a doubt. However, I created my own doubts about this calling, applying all human objections I could think of: *I'm a girl, I'm too old, I have a family; I'm a caregiver for my parents and brother;* yada, yada, yada…But it seemed that every objection I voiced God placed an even stronger call upon me that overcame these objections. So I did what I was instructed to do: I answered that call and changed my major in seminary to Divinity, and officially began studies for the ministry, totally unaware of the complex issues engulfing our future ministries.

When I was growing up, I thought most women going into ministry entered as missionaries, Christian educators and youth ministers. There were very few women entering ministry as pastors. As a matter of fact, I had never even heard of a woman pastor when I was growing up, although there must have been a few. In America, the Methodist church first began ordaining women in about 1956[8]. Still, it remained a mostly male-dominated position. Most folks going into the pastoral ministry back in those days were young men. Rarely were the folks entering ministry bi-vocational, part time or second career, and certainly not women!

I remember when my brother graduated from high school. He and a group of his friends went off to college to study for the ministry. After graduation from college, they went to seminary. Back then, it only took three years of seminary for the Bachelor of Divinity degree, a degree later changed, along with the requirements to satisfy it, to the Master of Divinity. During seminary, they worked with their district superintendent and their congregation back home and were interviewed and received their license to preach. Then, after graduation from seminary, they were ordained by their bishop. One of our friends had the bishop come to his church to ordain him. Their road into ministry was a spiritual journey and they were encouraged all along the way by their bishop, DS, pastor, and congregation. The process was more spiritual and personal than it is today, a lot less complicated and much less political.

As in everything, over the years to follow, things changed. The process into ministry began to evolve into a complicated journey and a journey that would be easy for the men and a more complicated for most of the women. Some of us have been singled out as "trouble-makers" because we follow the rules of our

---

[8] Ibid; ***Book of Discipline of the United Methodist Church***

denomination and attempt to lead our congregations according to those rules; some have been told that they needed to lose weight before they could be ordained; some have encountered lost paperwork, cancelled appointments, delays in scheduling needed appointments, and lost reference requests and letters, negative evaluations, to mention a few. In addition, all entering candidates for ministry must undergo a battery of psychological testing and interviews to prove they are "fit" for ministry; yet those who entered before this rule came into force did not have this requirement. For me, my journey into ministry was long and difficult with multiple obstacles and hurdles to overcome. My male counterparts seemed to fly through the maze of requirements on their way to certification and licensure much faster and with less scrutiny than several of us women in the group.

The candidacy process is now an organized system of hoops through which one must jump in order to be interviewed, nominated, voted on, and approved by a body of people who do not know you or anything about you or your passion for ministry. Each candidate must undergo a battery of psychological testing and a lengthy interview with a psychologist, as well as a multitude of background examinations and references. After all of this is completed, the common denominator in this group, the one who can sway the vote in favor of or against the candidate is the DS. So, if the DS (Supervising Clergy; SC) is a godly man or woman and recognizes the candidate's gifts and graces for ministry, things should move along well. However, if the SC has another agenda, the process could be detrimental to the candidate's ministry process. This happened to me at my home church while I was still a seminary student and it happened again at Tiny Town.

I recently re-read a book written under the pen name of Gregory Wilson, called **The Stained Glass Jungle**[9]. While no one knows for sure who the actual author is, this book was written about an ordained minister who became a DS in one of the southern conferences, and the politics he became involved in during his ministry and time as a DS in the 1960's. The author himself was an ordained minister who actually experienced these events during his ministry. This is not a new problem and it is not found only in our denomination. Where there are people struggling for control and power, there will be politics and ungodly behaviors of varying degrees involved in that journey.

I found politics at every turn. It has been as if the fire of the Holy Spirit was burning within me giving me this strong passion for ministry while others were constantly pouring water on me, trying to put the fire out! I found this true of one of my congregations and SC's who were actually supposed to be helping that fire burn brighter!

As I reflect on the beginning, I was so blessed to have a supportive and loving home church even though we had our problems with Larry. It will always be special to me and our friends there will always be our family. We love going back for worship and singing. The atmosphere is warm and friendly and we are welcomed as family. That will never change.

In addition, I was blessed beyond measure to be able to spend many years in my first appointment with the wonderful folks there. I learned how to be a pastor at that church; as a matter of fact, I learned so much from the members there. Our oldest

---

[9] **The Stained Glass Jungle;** Gregory Wilson; Doubleday and Company; 1962

member was about ninety-four years old when we arrived there. She always smiled and had some words of wisdom which I always listened to and took to heart! Since I was in seminary when I started there, the members took pride in "grading" my preaching. At first they felt strange saying anything negative, but were reassured that an honest evaluation would help me grow. They lovingly gave me pointers and advice and I appreciated each and every word. I will never forget the place they played in my early formation as a minister and pastor.

As it became time to move on to my second appointment, I was blessed to take with me the love and support of two wonderful congregations and many happy memories!

3

Ministry as Calling

"...I urge you to live a life worthy of the calling you have received. Be completely humble and gentle; be patient, bearing with one another in love. Make every effort to keep the unity of the Spirit through the bond of peace" (Ephesians 4:1, NIV).

The term "calling" is familiar to ministers, church and lay leaders. We tend to use that term frequently and I wonder if we truly understand its meaning. According to the scripture, "calling" really has a straightforward meaning: calling out to someone or something; catching someone or something's ear for a reason. If we look in the Old Testament in the first chapter of Genesis, God called the light day. Here, "to call" means "to name" and "to name" means to call something into being. It is a form of making. So when we speak of "Calling", we mean that we are called by God "to be".

When we look at this term further, we see that it actually could be a synonym for salvation. It is God's calling out to his people and calling them unto himself. In the Bible, calling is one of the central themes. Throughout the Old Testament, God called

His people. In the New Testament, Jesus called his disciples, called his followers, and called each of us into service.

To be technical about this topic and to clearly understand it, we will discuss the two forms of calling here. Our primary calling is to God and not to something like motherhood, or nursing or teaching. Our secondary calling, then, is our answer to God's call upon our lives to serve him in all that we think, speak, live and act. When we answer God's call upon our lives, he places within us the gifts we will need to accomplish that calling. He will never send us out unprepared.

When God, through the action of His Spirit, calls men and women into ministry, it is the Holy Spirit who has called, set aside, appointed and anointed that person for ministry, not a committee, an individual, or a group of earthly strangers. At the same time, those who are called are blessed with moral and spiritual power, and are anointed by the Holy Spirit as God's prophet in the church—His Biblical Officer. This biblical officer refuses to compromise biblical principles. They have no biblical right to be autocratic, dictatorial or domineering (1 Peter 5: 1-4). No person of God who is filled with the Spirit will manifest such an attitude. By the same token, when God has ordained, appointed and anointed His ministers, no earthly being has the power to terminate this union: *What God has joined together, let man not separate (Matthew 19:6)*. While this passage specifically speaks to marriage, the point is well taken: What God creates and blesses in heaven belongs to Him and only He can end it.

All clergy called of God are ministers of the Gospel until God decides that they are not. We may change churches or denominations, but that does not change the fact that we are equipped to serve, we are educated to teach and preach, and we are "Reverend" before God. This is how I was prepared for ministry in seminary. This ideal, perfect way that God has prepared the ones He has called, becomes less than perfect and confusing when we enter the human factor and allow worldly agendas to interfere with God's agenda for our lives.

Ministry is a gift. A minister is one who ministers by the Word and one who ministers through helps. The gift of ministry puts a person into the ministry and equips them with the supernatural ability to minister to the spiritual needs of others, by the Word of God, for the perfecting of the saints and the perfecting of ministry, and for the edification of the Body of Christ (Ephesians 4: 11-17; Acts 6: 2-4; 20: 24; Romans 12:7; 1 Timothy 1:12).

The Bible specifically speaks to special characteristics of a minister. The Bible says that a minister is affectionate to one another, possesses brotherly love, responsibility and compassion; works without praise of man and is a servant of servants (Matthew 20: 20-28). There are several Spiritual Gifts that God places within each minister He calls. Of course, some may have more than others, but there are several that almost all ministers have if they have been truly called of God and equipped for ministry through His grace:

1. **The gift of faith:** the supernatural ability to believe and expect great things from God; the capacity to see what God is doing or wants to do in a given situation, and that God will do it even though it looks difficult or impossible. *It is yielded-ness.*

2. **The gift of knowledge:** the supernatural ability to know things by the revelation and illumination of the Holy Spirit as it applies to the study of the Word of God. It is the power to understand the universal and timeless truths of God and to link them with the church in its mission through Christ for justice and righteousness in the world. *It is Humility.*
3. **The gift of wisdom:** the supernatural ability to critically evaluate and employ knowledge. It is the ability to make concrete and specific applications of divine knowledge received directly from God, from one's spiritual gift of knowledge, or from another's shared gift or gifts. *It is fear of the Lord.*
4. **The gift of prophecy:** the gift and motivation to preach and proclaim the Word of God. It is the supernatural ability to link biblical truths with God's will for today's living and to be an instrument for revealing or interpreting previous or current messages from God for righteous and just living in today's world. *It is truthfulness.*
5. **The gift of evangelist:** the supernatural ability to preach to lost sinners, their judgment, their eternal destiny, and their need for salvation: to give such witness to the love of God as expressed in Jesus Christ that it moves others to accept that love and to become Disciples of Christ. *It is love, patience and understanding.*
6. **The gift of government:** the supernatural ability to organize, administer and lead the activities of others in the accomplishment of common goals. It manifests itself in organizing and coordinating persons and materials

effectively to reach objectives and goals consistent with God's plan for the church; a leader of church affairs; the ability to take criticism; one who is capable of appointing others to positions of authority. *It is leadership and shepherding the flock.*[10]

The above gifts are basic to ministry. Most ministers who are called of God and equipped by Him have many other gifts in addition to these mentioned.

God's people are a called people, and there are no exceptions. In Romans 11:29 Paul says, "God's gifts and His call are irrevocable". He is talking about God's ongoing care and concern for His chosen people, the Jews. However, the scriptures teach that God pours out His gifts on every member of the Body of Christ (1 Corinthians 12:7), that God singles out each one of us for eternal fellowship with His Son, Jesus Christ (2 Thessalonians 2: 13-14).

God's call, like His gifts, comes in many forms (1 Peter 4:10). At different times we are called in different ways, which means that God's call is not a once-in-a-lifetime event. It is an ongoing process, endlessly varied according to our need and God's purpose. So, to what does God call us? God calls us first to salvation. Secondly, God calls us to holiness—to yielded-ness; to turn from the ways of the world and to live a holy and pure life. Third, God calls us to ministry—all Christians are called to be servants and to minister—some are called by God to be shepherds—but all are called to minister. And, fourth, God calls

---

[10] Information learned from lectures and discussion; Doctor of Ministry, Pastoral Leadership degree. *Doctrine of the Holy Spirit*

us to community—to belonging to Jesus as the Body of Christ, and to be in community with each other as that Body.

We are called by God and blessed with Spiritual Gifts. We are to use these gifts to glorify Him. When we fail to do this or when we prevent someone else from using their gifts, we sin. When we sin we grieve the Holy Spirit, and we are commanded in the Scripture to *"Grieve not the Holy Spirit of God"* (Ephesians 4:30, KJV)[11].

Traits of a Minister

The servant of Jesus Christ lives in humility to Christ. The minister of the Gospel of Jesus Christ ought to have two very basic traits. They should have the trait of being servant and slave of Jesus Christ (Phil. 2: 6-11), the number one focus. "I serve the risen Lord!" The second trait he/she should have is that of true humility. In the Scriptures, Jude meets both of these. Humility is nothing to boast about. As a matter of fact, if you boasted about humility, it would be a contradiction. But some Christians do take pride in being humble. When you take pride in being humble you scare away a lot more fish than you catch.

This reminds me of a story that I heard that goes like this: The little boy was out fishing with only a switch for a pole and a bent pin for a hook. But, in spite of his limitations, he was catching many fish. A city fellow, who had spent a lot of time fishing with very little success who also thought he had the best fishing outfit,

---

[11] Scripture quotations marked KJV are taken from the Holy Bible, The King James Version Reference Bible, copyright © 1996 by Broadman & Holman Publishers. Used by permission of Broadman & Holman Publishers. All rights reserved.

came across the little fellow with his long string of fish. He asked the boy the reason of his success. The boy said, "Sir, the secret of it all is that I had to keep myself out of sight!"

I say that to say this: we must keep ourselves out of sight if we are to be a blessing to others. The true minister is the one who humbles himself or herself, who surrenders to Jesus Christ as a slave, and serves Him. True ministers are sanctified, set apart by God, and only God. The foundation of Christian service does not rest upon such man-made things as human credentials, schools, papers or commendations! As helpful as these things may be, they are not the foundation of our service to Christ. The foundation for service is Christ and the great work Christ has called us to do!!

Characteristics of a Minister

1. *He is commissioned by God alone* (Galatians 1:1): There are people who questioned God's call upon Paul; they questioned if he'd really been called by God to be a minister. What they were doing, however, is that they were set on destroying Paul's, ministry. The reasons why are because he was different and had not followed the "regular process" for entering the ministry, because he preached a different message, and because he bypassed the normal way of doing things by following Scripture and God instead of man.

Paul made it clear that he was called by God into the ministry and that he was not called by men or of men. No man made him fit for the ministry and he was not made a minister by man. His call into the ministry was by Jesus Christ and God the Father. His call came from the highest source possible: from both God the Father and God the Son.

Many times to this day, critics cause trouble for the ministers of God. Ministers must boldly declare their call into ministry—not in a boastful or supra-spiritual way, but in a humble and clear way. Every minister must examine his heart and make sure his call into ministry has been commissioned by God! God has placed us in the court room of the world to defend the gospel of Christ. You see, the ministry is not a profession to be chosen, a job to earn a living, a position to secure recognition and esteem, a servants agency founded by man, a call of men or by men. The ministry is of God! Only God can give a true call and commission into the ministry.

Paul was recognized by "the brothers" (other ministers). A true brother or sister in Christ is more than a friend. The "brothers" recognized him and knew his call and ministry. No matter what we do to the brethren, we are doing it unto Jesus Christ. When critics attack the minister, it is time for true brothers and sisters in the Lord to step forward and support him/her in their ministry and declare the truth in the Lord. True brothers (and sisters) defend and come to the aid of a brother or sister when he/she is criticized and attacked. Jesus said in John 15:13 "Greater love hath no man than this, than a man lay down his life for his friends."

Jeremiah 1:5 sums this up nicely as it states "The believer's call into ministry is of God and not of yourself". Anyone who attempts to undermine the ministry of one called of God sins against God!

2. ***He wishes the very best for other believers*** (Galatians 1:3): Paul wanted the Galatians to experience the Grace of God. God is Love and makes it possible for man to experience His love and grace. Grace comes before peace. So many in the church had fallen from the Grace of God: they were complaining, causing trouble in the church, leading divisiveness throughout the church, and finding fault with Paul's ministry. He wanted everyone to come to know the Grace of God by coming to know Jesus Christ as their Savior and Lord. He wanted everyone to know the Peace of God as they confronted their struggles in their walk through life. Paul said that if you are depending on works of any kind to save you then you have fallen from the sphere of God's Grace! That is what the phrase "falling from grace" means: depending on some other means for salvation other than the Grace of God.

Every minister should wish the very best for other believers— even for his critics and enemies. It might be difficult but the very call into the ministry is to recognize the very grace and peace of God. Do you help others see the grace and peace of God as they walk through this life?

3. ***A true minister proclaims the work of Christ*** (Galatians 1: 4-5): Christ gave himself for our sins; Christ came to deliver us from this sinful and evil world; God willed it—wills us to be saved (1 Tim 2: 4-6; Matt 20: 28); the result of Jesus' death is the glory of God.

4. ***A true minister preaches against those who turn against the true Gospel and the preachers who preach and teach any other gospel*** (Galatians 1: 6-9). Protect the innocent sheep against the evil wolves. God has only one Gospel and that is the Gospel of Jesus Christ: God's Gospel is the only message!

5. ***A true minister seeks to please God not men*** (Galatians 1:10-16). The true minister's life becomes radically changed through Jesus Christ. The critics of Paul said he was inconsistent; that he was trying to please both God and man. They said that the Gospel He preached was false. They said that His ministry was false and that He only used the ministry to please others and His own agenda. He became all things to all people. It is a very easy thing to seek to please men instead of God. The Gospel we proclaim can become tainted with our own agenda and our lifestyle can offend as we set our hearts toward pleasing men instead of God. This will happen unless we show by our example that our lives are changed. Always seek to please God and be a blessing to man. One cannot be a genuine minister of the Gospel and attempt to please people by compromising the truths of the Gospel (1 Cor. 4: 3-6). Paul regarded his duty to speak "not as pleasing men, by God, which trieth our hearts". All believers of the Gospel of Christ must make it their aim, as did Paul, to please God even if it means displeasing some people. Paul had a conversion and a radical change of life (Gal. 1: 13-16): Paul previously persecuted the church of God. He struck out against the early believers more than anyone

else (Acts 9: 3-4). The point is this: if you want to do something against Jesus do it to the church. If you want to do something for Jesus, do it to the church!

6. ***The true minister follows God in his life*** (Galatians 1: 17-24). It is our calling to bear a captivating testimony for Christ. One of the most powerful tools of witnessing is your personal testimony. The life of the believer should become so strong that it is obvious in the life of the believer. Paul was under attack by some of the critics of the churches of Galatia. They were saying that he was not a God-called preacher and that he was preaching false gospel. They sowed the poison of gossip. They said he was in the ministry only as a profession and for what he could get out of it. However, Paul was proven to be a God-called preacher and that his call and his message did come from God and his message was the true message of the Lord Jesus Christ. In fact, he never received the Gospel from anyone other than Jesus Christ Himself. Paul sought to learn the truth from God and God alone. Paul followed God first in his life—he did not follow men. The true minister follows God in his/her life.

Support the Minister in Word and Deed

All members of the Body of Christ should support the minister in word and deed (Galatians 4: 12-20). One of the most important duties of the minister is in bringing back the lost sheep; to restore sheep that have strayed away from the Lord. Backsliding people need appeal after appeal, for they are walking a dangerous walk when they turn their backs to God. These persons are usually alienated from their pastor. They want little to do with the minister when they are turning away from God. False prophets tear down the minister's character and ministry every chance they get. All members should restore their affection and respect for the preachers of God.

The Bible is clear as to how the Body of Christ is to treat ministers of God.

1. Treat the minister of God as a "brother/sister". (Galatians 4: 12). Paul pleaded with the congregation to support him and minister with him and not turn their backs on him. Congregants, we must love and show kindness to those who are against us and we must pray for our pastors. Preachers, we must pray for our congregations, also.
2. Welcome true preachers of God (Galatians 4: 13-16). They:
   A. should be welcomed in their witness
   B. should be welcomed even in their infirmity
   C. should be welcomed in the truth they proclaim

How many churches turn against their pastors because they tell the truth? Pastors get spiritually tarred and feathered for preaching the truth. Because of this, many end up preaching what their congregations want to hear instead of what the Word actually says. Preach the truth in love and not out fear of retaliation or rejection!

3. Guard against and reject false preachers (Galatians 4:17). False teachers attempt to alienate the people of the church from the pastor. The true teachers focus the people of God and on God himself.
4. Receive true preachers always (Galatians 4: 18-20). The church should always accept preachers who labor for the church's welfare.
   A. true preachers hold each believer in his heart as children of God
   B. true preachers agonize over the growth of believers... they want believers living and growing in Christ.
   C. true preachers guard the church against error. The true preacher protects the believers from false teachers and wrong doing. And, a true preacher of God protects the vision of Christ and His church.

I want to close this chapter out by mentioning what the Bible says about false preachers, teachers and lay members of our congregations. I mention this because, as you will see in the following chapters, many of the lay leadership of Tiny Town Church and the clergy leadership fall into this group.

False Teachers, Preachers and Lay Members of the Church

Preacher, church member, you yourself must make sure that you are genuine—that you yourself are not a heretic...a wolf in sheep's clothing. They appear on the outside to be real but on the inside they are ravenous wolves. Ask yourself: Am I sure that I am real. Every false preacher claims to be real but he does not preach the absolute truth (Matt. 7:17): They appear to be messengers of life and they appear real, innocent and good. But, they lack two things: a life and a testimony changed by God. They are out for self and personal gain. They are concerned with realizing their own motives for getting ahead. They want their own following and want people to praise them and look up to them. They seek power and fame. They use all the media they can but they never preach the true gospel of the living Lord. False preachers have not been put in the ministry by God, but by themselves. They are out for themselves only. What makes a preacher true or false? It is what that person believes about Jesus Christ: You must walk in the Spirit; you cannot be in the Spirit and love not your brother and sister. You cannot be in the spirit and be also in the flesh. A true preacher confesses truth always. He confesses always that Jesus Christ is the Son of God and came to earth to save man. They are indwelt by the Spirit of God himself and this is obvious by the life they live and the way they love others.

Do you know anyone like this in your church? False teachers are not God-called teachers. They choose to teach in the church as a way to serve people. They are full of charm and they are good administrative people, full of grace and very friendly. False teachers are destined to judgment because they do not teach the Word of God and, instead, teach false doctrines and self-motives.

While they may not seem like it, false teachers are ungodly people. They turn the grace of God into lasciviousness. They are not pure, just or loving. They are lost and unsaved, deceptive and lead people away from Christ. They are immoral because they practice open and shameless indecency, crossing boundaries either sexually or emotionally. They murmur, grumble and complain against things of God. God likens that to Spiritual adultery.

How many grumble and gossip in the church because they are not happy with what God has given them; they are not happy with their spiritual leadership that has been given by God? We ought to be happy with what God is doing in our lives. But how many are unhappy and cause trouble? Believers often feel that God expects too much of them—that they are missing out on things in the world. They also feel that God will forgive them if they slip and partake of these things. And God will forgive a genuine confession if one is made, because 1 John 7:9 does say this. But your freedom in grace stops when you go further that God says you can go!

False teachers are carnal Christians, and have thoughts and dreams of grandeur and engage in the pleasures of the world. They do not struggle to keep their thoughts clean and pure and they dream and covet after positions and possessions and things of the world. They speak evil of dignities—we are told to pray for those who are our leaders, but the false teachers speak evil about them. They reject authority; they do not follow the laws of God or the church. They flaunt their power and they scoff at spiritual beings and Christ's followers who are striving to live holy lives.

It is sad to say, but false teachers go in the way of Cain (1 John 3:11): the way of unbelief; they do not believe that they have to go the way of God exactly as God says; they go astray; they seek power, control, things of the world, and lead people into destruction and sin for their own power and benefit. False teachers follow the way of rebellion and rejection of authority. They rebel against and reject the authority of God, and the ministers God has appointed and placed in His church (Jude 11-12). And, most of all, they reject the supreme authority of Christ Himself. They refuse to go the way of Christ and choose to use the church and its people for their own end. They are spots and blemishes upon the fellowship of the church.

They cause division in the fellowship of the church and its people and cause the destruction of the Spirit of Christ among them. They show little concern for what they are doing to the congregation and the fellowship there and care only about promoting their programs and agenda for their own selfish reasons and gain. I experienced this personally at Tiny Town Church, as you will see in the chapters ahead.

False teachers will be judged: they will be judged for all of their ungodly deeds (Matthew 16: 27), and they will be judged for all of the untrue, defiant words spoken against Christ and Christ's ministers. These false teachers are murmurers and complainers because they don't have the peace of God in their hearts and lives. They are truly dissatisfied with life and especially their life. A false teacher has flattery speech and words that are empty. They have flattery speech and empty words because what they say is not of God. They are empty and unstable. They flatter people for personal gain and are serving under the umbrella of Christianity. They do that to make a living. They know nothing about God's call into the ministry (1 John 3:16). They flatter in order to win favor and get what they want in the church or in their position in the church. This leads to favoritism in the church which permeated Tiny Town Church. The world is filled with deception and lies. Those of the world always look for things wrong in the church so they can do things their way and take control. They always divide the church. The division, then, is between mature believers and those who follow false teachers.

At Tiny Town Church, you will see how Jodie was a false teacher. There were many before her at this church, but after she became a member there, her personality was so strong that she dominated the others and took control. She took control of the Supervising Clergy and Pastor Kim and soon the three of them became triangulated in an unforgivable relationship that was aimed at control, destruction and hiding secrets. Her personality was so strong that she fooled Alyce, Pastor Kim, Bertha, Cathy, and Crystal into believing that what she said was true.

Believers must defend and propagate the faith and resist false teaching in four ways: first by building themselves up in the most holy faith; the holy faith is the NT revelation handed down by Christ and the Apostles (2 John 3). This requires the study of God's Word and a determined effort to know the truth and teachings of Scripture (Acts 2: 42). Secondly, by praying to the Spirit: we must pray by the enabling power of the Holy Spirit by looking to the Holy Spirit to inspire, guide, energize, sustain, and help us to do battle in our praying. Praying in the Spirit includes both praying with one's mind and praying with one's spirit. Third, by remaining in the sphere of God's love for us: This involves loyal obedience to God and His Word (John 15: 9-10). And fourth, by looking for and awaiting the return of our Lord and the eternal glory that will accompany His return (John 14:2; Jude 17-25).

Christians, we must guard against deceivers. There are many deceivers in this world. There have been since the beginning of time. They are in our churches, for sure. These are imposters who do not live holy lives. The mission of a deceiver is to deceive. They are an agent of Satan (the devil) and they try to convince you that the devil is not real. They do not live a holy life. They do not love their brother or sister[12]. Any person can be a deceiver, even the sweet little old lady, weak and frail, who attends church each Sunday; even the ones who teach Bible studies, or the ones who give large sums of money to the church, or those who work with our children and youth, or even the ones who lead the church and supervise the clergy.

Who is sitting in the pew next to you? Who is in your pulpit?

---

[12] Information learned from lectures and discussions; Master of Arts, Christian Leadership and Master of Divinity degrees, Doctor of Ministry, Pastoral Leadership degree; *The Study of 1, 2, 3 John-Jude and Galatians.*

4

Satan's Seven plus Two

"Whosoever hateth his brother is a murderer: and ye know that no murderer hath eternal life abiding in him. Hereby perceive we the love of God, because he laid down his life for us: and we ought to lay down our lives for the brethren" (1John 3: 15-16, KJV).

The time came for me to leave my little church in the country and the wonderful people there, and move on to another ministry setting. I was appointed to a beautiful little church in a tiny little town not far away. I will call it Tiny Town Church, Small Town, America, because what happened there could happen in any small town and in any small rural fellowship or church.

As we prepare to enter to the period of this story that I call *"the desert"*, I feel that I should introduce you to the group who were the active trouble-makers, the ones who played an instrumental role in the trouble at Tiny Town. I think this is important to clearly understand before we dive into the story. I will introduce you to the characters in the order of their appearance in the story, for lack of a better way, and not in the order of importance or impact on the sequence of events that happened.

"Satan's Seven" consists of "Pastor Kim", "Dusty", "Jodie", "Bertha", "Cathy", "Crystal", and "Diane". The "Plus Two" consists of "Alyce" and his supervisor, "Adam". These are not their real names and their basic positions in the church have been altered to prevent any identification.

Let me deviate here and clarify my thoughts on Satan and the Devil. I have come to refer in a very general sense to Satan as Satan. However, in a more detailed sense, I believe that Satan is the supreme evil, the Antichrist as referred to in the Scriptures. The devil, on the other hand, is one of Satan's warriors, and there are a multitude working overtime to achieve Satan's plan here on this earth. At Tiny Town I encountered seven devils in the church plus two who were clergy management. Anyone who has their own agenda and tries to destroy the ministry of the church and the one whom God has commissioned as His minister, sins against God, and because of this, are out of fellowship with God. This is how Satan achieves his goal of destroying faith and ministry among God's people. As I said before, this is not unique to Tiny Town. Satan is alive in many churches and working overtime to destroy them and the people who worship there.

Alyce

The first one of these players I was introduced to was Alyce. I spoke to Alyce very briefly one April afternoon, by telephone, where he offered me the position at Tiny Town Church. The conversation was brief and was over before I knew it. The content of his conversation was to request that I send him a resume so he could forward it on to the church. After that brief conversation, my contact with him was limited. Alyce ended up being one of the main characters in this story. He had the power and position to do great things at Tiny Town but ended up selling out to Satan just to hide his secrets.

Alyce was a controlling womanizer, and he didn't hesitate to use both his influence and affluence to his advantage. He became my Supervising Clergy when I moved to Tiny Town. He was to be my supervisor, so to speak, but mainly my resource person and my pastor, my spiritual guide. I can honestly say that I had never encountered anyone like him before. He worshiped in our congregation only twice during my pastorate there. The first visit occurred about two months after my arrival. During the "meet and greet" time during the worship service, I noticed him hugging Jodie and the other women members of the "Seven". I avoided him totally and went down the outside isle of the sanctuary to greet the congregants. However, after the worship, I was greeting the congregants as they made their way out of the sanctuary when Alyce came up to me to speak to me and my family. I held out my hand to shake his and he grabbed me in a frontal squeeze. I immediately pushed away to prevent the completion of the squeeze. He looked at me and moved on to hug the other women. He grabbed my elderly mother, but mom swung her walker between her and him to block the embrace. Yea mom!! The old gal is pretty sharp at 90! Our response sent a clear message that we did not approve of crossing boundaries. However, this event just added to the ongoing emotional trauma I had begun suffering at the hands of my beloved church.

Coming into Tiny Town I had glowing evaluations from previous meetings with the ministry committees, prior SC's, and Church PPRC's. However, over the eleven months there, Alyce publicly ridiculed and mocked my achievements, the church's progress, and my ability to manage, every chance he got. It was apparent to me and the congregation that he had nothing nice to say about the church or their new pastor. It seemed to be a problem to him that I came in with more education than he had and he verbally made note of this fact in our Charge Conference meeting soon after my arrival, bringing embarrassment to me and my church members. He repeatedly crossed emotional and professional barriers with me by interfering with nearly every decision I made in the management of my charge and threatening me, telling me he was keeping a file on me and a record of what I was doing. Soon I realized that someone in the congregation must be keeping him informed of everything going on in the administration of the church; which, I might add, was strictly by the book. He confessed that it was Jodie. Of course, none of what Jodie was feeding Alyce was accurate or the truth, but he believed it because he just did not like me or the congregation of that church. In fact, he admitted that he encouraged Satan's Seven and others to bypass the pastor and the proper church committees and bring all complaints and concerns directly to him, violating the rules and regulations set forth in the **Book of Discipline of the United Methodist Church.**[13]

---

[13] Information taken from personal files and records of Tiny Town Church, as well as extensive interviews of current and past members of the church. All information used with written permission of those interviewed.

Pastor Kim

The second player I had the opportunity to meet was Pastor Kim, the outgoing pastor of Tiny Town. During the course of the transition from her pastorate to mine, I had many, many phone calls and emails from her. Pastor Kim used her position and power to get into all of the personal lives and business of the congregants at Tiny Town and then gossip about them to others, especially Alyce, her supervising clergy. Because she was single and lonely, she formed an instant friendship with Alyce. They went on mission trips together and she involved him in her day to day decisions concerning pastoring at Tiny Town Church. He was seen by other congregants crossing boundaries with Pastor Kim and it was obvious that their relationship interfered with Alyce's objective supervision of Tiny Town Church. In addition, Pastor Kim formed alliances with the other six members of this group of devils in order to secure her position at the church. She became very close to Jodie and gave Jodie all of the pastor's office responsibilities to do, so that she could have the time to have a social life outside the church. She stacked the committees of the church with these loyal cohorts so that this small group essentially ran the church and other members were not allowed to serve in the church in leadership positions. Most of the members began to leave the church. Those who remained and who were not among her inner circle, rebelled and tried to make things right. But this effort was to no avail.

Pastor Kim's relationship in the community and church saddened me greatly. She felt no remorse for her appearance, not as a minister of the Gospel of Jesus Christ, but rather that of a "call-girl", which my husband and I discovered on our first meeting with her prior to our arrival there. I found her appearance very distracting to say the least. Having to look past cleavage and plunging jewelry, we found it difficult to concentrate on our discussion with her at the dinner table. As a matter of fact, one of our congregants later told me that he and his grandson saw Pastor Kim walking her dogs down the highway wearing very short shorts, and, according to the unsuspecting onlookers, displaying an appearance unbecoming a representative of Christ and His church. During our visit, she talked non-stop about the many programs she had started at the church as well as how many children she had baptized over the last several years. This prideful conversation was all about her!

I would find out after my arrival that Pastor Kim failed to follow the **Book of Discipline** at all in any of her decisions but especially in her baptizing children who were unchurched and without parental consent and instruction. I even found several she had confirmed who were not yet baptized and others who were baptized at another Methodist church nearby but were baptized again at Tiny Town. In addition to all of this, Pastor Kim attempted to sway my attitudes against certain members of the congregation in order to promote her agenda and to keep her programs viable after I arrived there. She repeatedly attempted, through emails and phone calls prior to my arrival at Tiny Town, to demonize and discredit certain members of the congregation to protect her own agenda and the agenda of Satan's Seven so that they would retain control of the church. She spent many hours on the phone trying to convince me to bypass the rules of the local church as stated in the **Book of Discipline**, and go directly to

Alyce concerning members of the congregation she had previously discussed with him, thereby bypassing the proper committees. Both Pastor Kim and Jodie spent endless hours describing in detail their special friendship with Alyce and Jodie went so far as to say that if she doesn't get her way about something all she has to do is to call "her boy" Alyce and he'll take care of it.

During the first few months of my new appointment, Jodie parked herself in my office every day, spilling the beans on poor Pastor Kim and her management of Tiny Town Church. I knew what she was doing; Jodie was attempting to sway me to be her loyal cohort, like Pastor Kim, so that she would be able to continue her power trip as before. She was scared to death that her trip was about to end. But what she did was this: Jodie began to tell me how Pastor Kim only wanted to move up the success ladder in the church, which was obvious to me. She also told me that Pastor Kim padded the figures on the church reports to make it look like there were more members than actually were; to make it look like the church was growing by listing all of the "programs" she had begun; by inflating the baptism and new members numbers and not updating the membership list to reflect accurate church numbers. Pastor Kim played right in to the "Seven's" plan of control and for eight years she nearly destroyed that little church. Finally, in a last ditch effort to reclaim their church, the leadership and members pitched such a fit and the situation at Tiny Town got so bad that Alyce was forced to move Pastor Kim to another district many miles away. It was this decision for which I would pay a heavy price.

Alyce and the remaining "Six" were extremely angry about the situation. They were angry mostly at the church and they became angry at me before I ever arrived. I had no idea that this was the situation at Tiny Town when I was placed there.

Dusty

I met Dusty at Tiny Town when my husband and I went to get introduced to the "Pastor's Committee" at Tiny Town about two or three weeks prior to our arrival. Dusty didn't say much at all. He was a quiet guy so it was hard to tell if he was just being nice or if he was actually in agreement with what was being said. Dusty proved to be an all right sort of guy but one who had a long history in that church, was a very large financial giver, and could never say "no". He was an enabler and he enabled all of the bad behaviors of the rest of the group when he had the power and position to correct the situation.

Jodie

Even though I spoke to Jodie on the phone several times prior to my arrival at Tiny Town, which I thought was very unusual, I didn't meet her until we met with the "Pastor's Committee". The first time I spoke on the phone with Jodie, she introduced herself to me as the church's "Administrative Assistant". She said it was her job to handle all of the office duties and bulletins. I immediately thought how strange, but fortunate, it was to have an administrative assistant in a church as small as Tiny Town. I wondered how much that was costing the church and could they even afford it! Later, I would find out the truth about Jodie. Jodie was truly an evil person. After Pastor Kim left and I arrived, it was

The Devil Made Them Do it at Tiny Town Church

Jodie who hung on to the control of the church with all her might. She had the loudest mouth, was on every committee and controlled every program that was in existence at that church. She effectively ran off more congregants than anyone else I had ever seen in all my days as a member of a church. She manipulated every person she could, especially the elderly who were a little weak-minded. She maintained a close relationship with Pastor Kim after Pastor Kim left and she maintained a close relationship with Alyce on a personal level. When she did not get her way, she pledged to get even. She prided herself as the "lay delegate" to annual conference and used this as her means to maintain control over the church because the lay delegate gets to serve on most of the committees and have a voice in everything that goes on. Then, while on these committees, she would chase off the good folks and she and her buddies would maintain control of all of the activities and functions.

Jodie led all of the gossip. She had a gossip chain that covered the entire church, district, community and nearly the state! She talked about everything. She would take things and turn them around into lies. She made up stories about everyone who crossed her. If she didn't get her way, she would go to Alyce and tell him lies about that person, which he believed because of his relationship with Jodie, and then he would turn on that individual and make them the bad guy. Jodie could not tell the truth about anything. She was disruptive during worship, walking in and out during special moments of the service so she was sure to be noticed. She always sat on the third row. She was always the first to volunteer for everything.

Prior to my arrival at Tiny Town, we met with Jodie at her request. She wanted me to be sure and keep the youth program intact after my arrival. Apparently, Pastor Kim and Jodie had collected a group of unchurched, largely rowdy acting, delinquents, and brought them to the church and served them dinner each Wednesday evening. They would babysit these kids while their parents had their own activities going on, at the church's expense, and then label them their "youth group". I will admit that, if done properly following proper channels in the church, this group could have been a great area of ministry. However, they did not qualify as a youth group as outlined in the **Book of Discipline** and no formal classification as such had ever been made by the Administrative Board of the church. They did not attend Sunday school, church services or any of the functions of the church, and no one wanted to be their sponsors or counselors except Pastor Kim and Jodie. At the same time, the dinners were costing the church money, which they did not have in the budget.

I advised Jodie to leave things alone until I got there. I told her that it was unfair to ask me to make a decision on something before I had even moved there and looked into the situation myself. I wanted the opportunity to review this program and meet the kids involved. However, when I arrived, Jodie had suspended the program and then went to Alyce and told him that I had cancelled it. This was the first of the many programs of our church that Jodie dismantled because she didn't get what she wanted.

Soon after I arrived, I began making pastor calls on my congregation. I knew that there were problems but it was not until I began visiting the congregation in their homes that I discovered how each person saw Jodie as the center of the problems. When the time came for us to place into nomination folks who we thought would make good leaders for the upcoming church year,

I disclosed to the committee what the membership had said about Jodie being in control of the church. I advised them that it would be better to let someone else have the experience of serving as lay delegate. This would eliminate Jodie's hold on the church by removing her from most of the vital committees. When Jodie got wind of this, through a leak on the committee, she turned on me and told me that "whatever it took" she would "get even" with me and the church. From that day on, one by one, the programs of the church began to disappear. Break-ins in the church began to happen, doors were found mysteriously left open, a snake was found in the kitchen, prank phone calls were received on my personal phone, threatening phone calls began to come in, Jodie stalked me daily, sitting outside my house and church office all night watching my every move; my utility trailer was stolen out of the church driveway; church property was moved from the church to her house and placed in a yard sale without notice to the pastor; on and on and on. I was becoming afraid to walk from the office to the parsonage at night because she watched me all the time. I called the police but she was gone by the time they got there, so there was nothing that could ever be done to stop this behavior.

Jodie finally ended up leaving the church but continued to control it through her friends, the rest of Satan's Seven, who continued to stay there. I was afraid and I was emotionally stressed, to say the least, and I found myself without a supervisor that I felt was objective with whom I could discuss these problems.

Apparently, Jodie and her husband had a history of intimidating people if they did not get their way or what they thought they deserved. According to court documents, both had been in and out of court many, many times for "getting even" with others whom they felt had wronged them. Their evil antics usually resulted in destruction of the other person's property and their filing a lawsuit against Jodie and her husband. There were, however, several arrest warrants issued for assault and other bully crimes. This was enough to render me fearful of what she might resort to in order to get even with me and the church.

Satan and his warriors will do anything to destroy the saints of God. They will work endlessly to destroy the church, the church's mission, vision, and ministry, and they will never quit as long as we let them in. They will not rest until they destroy God's people and God's ministers.

Bertha

I do not know how male clergy begin their new jobs, but I began mine by cleaning. That first week I cleaned our file cabinets, dusted shelves cleaned windows, closets and cupboards. When I had finished my office, I began in the parsonage kitchen.

The next morning, I went to the post office to collect the mail. Mail had gathered in the post office box for well over a week, because that's the amount of time that had elapsed between the time Pastor Kim left and I arrived.

I went through the mail, not sure of exactly what to do with it. So I did what I had always done before: I sorted it in stacks and placed each stack in the proper inter-office box. All of the mail addressed to the church, I figured was mine. I opened each piece carefully and reviewed its contents. The statements from the bank or creditors were placed in the church treasurer's box to be processed or paid. And then I began to meet them, one by one. I began to meet Satan's Seven; and Bertha was number five!

Bertha had grown up in that church and, while not a very faithful member or supporter, she was the church treasurer. She told me that I was not to open any mail, especially the bills or bank statements. She told me that this church did not want me to know anything about the financial status of the church and that she answered only to the finance committee chairperson, not me, the pastor. Now, in the Methodist church, the pastor functions as the CEO/COO, and it is one of the duties of the pastor to clearly understand the financial status of the church he/she pastors. So, I knew that this was wrong.

On several occasions, I noticed Bertha and Jodie manipulating the finances of the church so I immediately figured that this was the reason they did not want me to see the bank statements. When questioned about this, I was told that they have the authority to manage the different accounts of the church and to decide where the money should be placed. I noticed that the money was being moved into the programs of the church controlled by Jodie. Bertha went right along with this and did what Jodie instructed.

I informed both of them that this would have to stop and the proper procedures for approving funding for projects would have to follow the proper channels. Almost immediately, any requests I made to the church treasurer were ignored totally or severely delayed. In addition to this, she became delinquent in paying church bills resulting in cancellation notices and missed and delinquent payment of the pastor's monthly salary and expenses. She made up stories about the church's condition and the reasons for nonpayment, all of which were not true. She refused to attend worship services but rather sat in the church office and worked on bookkeeping during services until I asked her to conduct business on another day, other than Sunday, the Lord's Day. Neither Bertha nor Jodie pledged financial support of the church.

    I brought both Bertha and Jodie into my office one afternoon to try to discuss the deteriorating relationship between them, me and our church, but instead of constructive discussion, Bertha boldly told me that she did not have to follow any rules in the church rule book (the **Book of Discipline of the Methodist Church**) or any other church rules. I reminded her that she signed church forms stating that she would comply with certain procedures as the church's treasurer and she needed to abide by these rules if she wanted to continue to serve the church in that capacity.

    I discussed this matter with Alyce who advised me to discuss this situation with the "pastor-parish committee chair and the finance committee chair, nominate another church treasurer for the new church year approaching, and call for Bertha's resignation immediately. Since it was already September and she only had three months until the year was out, I thought it would cause less pain if we just let the committee nominate someone else for the New Year and phase Bertha out peacefully at the end of her term. This is what we did.

    When good ole Bertha found out, through the weak link on the nominating committee (Cathy), that she was not going to be the church's treasurer in the upcoming year, it was as though the president of Fort Knox got fired! She was mad as a hornet. She called every member in the church. She was furious. I didn't tell anyone about her manipulating the church money; I did not tell anyone anything but that Alyce and I felt that it was time for someone else to have the opportunity to serve. She was so angry that she sent out a three page letter in her Christmas card to every member of the congregation. This letter blasted me up one side and down the other, calling me a liar and other things. This letter and card defamed my character so much so that it caused another nail in the coffin, so to speak.

I summoned Alyce to the church to meet with the congregation, hopefully in my support and in the support of his decision to replace Bertha; but that just did not happen. Instead, he came in to that meeting, where the congregation had gathered to hear reassuring words that their pastor was not this awful person that Bertha had claimed, telling that poor struggling group of people how awful they were. He said: "you people are terrible people"; he continued to ridicule them and scold them as if they had done something wrong. The culprits were Jodie and Bertha and as the meeting progressed, Bertha got angry at Alyce and told him that she didn't have to follow any rules and I can't write what was said next by Alyce or Bertha! It was awful. The meeting was void of the Holy Spirit! In a few short weeks, Bertha moved to another church.

Cathy

Cathy was an elderly lady who had been a member of that church for many years. She did not grow up in that church, but she did transfer from another church many years prior to my coming. Cathy was the queen of gossips. She gossiped about anything and everything to everyone. The sad thing was that she could not get stories straight and she ended up spreading rumors and gossip that were not true. She complained about everything and took all of her complaints directly to Alyce via Dusty, who listened intently to her and encouraged her to go to Alyce to discuss her concerns. Dusty even drove Cathy to the town where Alyce's office was located so she could meet with him. To my surprise, all of her complaints were about me. I couldn't figure out what I was doing that was wrong because no one would ever tell me. I was careful not to make changes in things at first because I wanted to build up my congregation's trust first. I was also cautious what I said to any one because I did not know who I could trust and who was spreading the gossip. I kept quiet and listened. Cathy was poison. She bragged about being able to get rid of pastors that she didn't like. Cathy never left the church while I was there and she remained one of the two insiders who kept the information going out to Jodie, who did leave the church. Later, ill health and personal issues began to consume her.

Crystal

Crystal also grew up in Tiny Town Church. Through the years she came and went before finally coming back to the church many years before I arrived. Crystal functioned as the church's lay leader. The Lay Leader is supposed to act as the head of the laity, the congregation, as they relate to the pastor. The pastor and the lay leader work closely together and the lay leader leads the worship and assists the pastor with other duties in the pastor's absence. When I arrived, Crystal was out sick. Because of this, I first met Crystal in the hospital on a routine pastoral visit. I then visited her at her home several times each week until her recovery. The long visits with Crystal and her husband at their home enabled them to meet and get to know their pastor. Her husband began coming to church for the first time ever!

Crystal functioned as a health care worker until her retirement so I understood her personality pretty well. It didn't take me long to figure out that she was really bossy and controlling. She had a close bond with Jodie and Cathy and these two kept Crystal full of gossip and lies about me and others; so much so that it consumed Crystal and kept her extremely angry all the time. Crystal was also searching for God in her life and stayed in conflict with the negativity being fed to her by Jodie and Cathy. It was obvious that she was being pulled in two different directions at once. She volunteered to lead Bible Studies as if it would help her sort out the strife she was dealing with in her own life. I liked Crystal in the beginning, but, for some unknown reason, she turned on me with a vengeance. We had a "called" meeting of the Administrative Board to discuss one of the programs of the church that she was passionate about. For some reason, she believed that I was trying to get rid of this program, when I was attempting to protect the church's interest and secure additional information about this program. I was quietly sitting across from her at the table as we discussed this information. She began screaming and cursing at me, spewing her spit in my face. I could not believe I was in the house of God. None of the others seated around the table could believe what they were hearing and seeing.

While she never left the church while I was there, she did find other reasons not to come to worship and support the functions. She came up with one excuse after another as to why she could not be present. What I came to find out was that Jodie was feeding

Crystal lies about me which Crystal believed and this kept her upset all the time. Gossip will kill a church, and it is evil!

Diane

Diane was an odd person. She just didn't quite seem to fit in. Diane was married to Dusty and each had their own separate lives even though they lived in the same house. Diane became a member of Tiny Town Church when she married Dusty. She served the church as Chairperson of various top level committees. This coincided with her private life as company leader.

Diane prided herself as being the largest financial donor to that church, even larger than her husband, Dusty. They both felt that a certain amount of power was awarded them for their generous giving. However, I was totally not impressed by this and they knew it because I did not seek their friendship or a special relationship with them as the others had done before me and as Alyce had done.

Diane was abrupt and rude to church members during board meetings often telling them to "shut up" and "sit down" when she thought they had spoken too long. She was a total control person, contradicting everyone who didn't agree with her, and hushing those who wanted to speak. She was famous for having the last word in everything and no one wanted to cross her or question what she said. The other congregants did not want to anger her for fear she would leave the church and take her money with her as she had threatened to do many times before.

When Bertha (her close friend and fellow member of Satan's Seven) called her to tell her that she was being replaced as the church treasurer for the upcoming year, Diane went ballistic. She called me on the church fellowship hall phone while I was in a meeting. I answered the phone and she spent about five straight minutes screaming at me at the top of her voice. She was so angry. She was angry because I had not consulted her before the nominating committee decided to replace Bertha. I told her, first of all that it was the committee' decision, not mine, to replace Bertha; and secondly, that it was not her place to be informed of this prior to the charge conference vote on the suggested nominees. I told her to nominate Bertha anyway at charge conference if she wanted her to serve. Then the membership could vote on who they wanted.

This incident was a clear example of control. Diane had placed her friends on these top committees so she could get what she wanted. When things started being conducted the proper way and the church started nominating and voting the proper way, those in control started to lose control and the old way of doing things began to fall apart.

Diane couldn't take this change so she finally went to another church. In spite of Diane's leaving and taking her money with her, and once the new officers took over at the beginning of the church year, attendance started to soar and financial giving right along with it. The congregation finally began to experience a peaceful church and the Holy Spirit moved among us at last!

Adam

Adam was the leader of the churches in that particular area. In our area, Adam was our ultimate leader; our Shepherd. I will go into Adam's role in this story in future chapters as well as why someone of this ranking is listed in this ungodly group. This may come as a surprise to many, but even leaders can be deceived by Satan and can have their own agendas at heart.

Leadership: we all want good leadership. We all want good Shepherds to lead us in and out of green pasture. We vote hoping to elect it, we apply for jobs hoping to work for it, and we go to school hoping to be educated by it. But we do not always find it. The trust we place in our leaders can be broken. So what are we to do? I think John 10 holds the answer and I want to discuss it briefly here.

In John 10, Jesus gives us a wonderful and vivid portrait of a shepherd caring for his sheep. The shepherd would lead his sheep out to distant areas and stay there for days. Being a good shepherd, he created a temporary corral, a pen to keep the sheep in when they were not grazing. Using the crude stones of the field, a shepherd could quickly put together such a structure and at night he would lay his body down in the opening of this corral, making himself the door. No sheep could wander away at night unless it stepped over the sleeping shepherd and no wolf could come in to do harm without waking the shepherd. He is the gate.

You see, more than any other duty, the goal of the shepherd is to protect the sheep. This is how you know a good shepherd from a bad shepherd. Does the shepherd/leader have the best interest of his/her people at heart? How do you know that he or she is a good shepherd? You know by looking at the sheep! Not all of the sheep appointed by Adam as pastors and supervisors had the people's best interest at heart. I encountered three who were filled with their own sinful desires, and those who are filled with their own sinful desires and agendas are a danger to their flock; and these are the pastors they supervise, and the congregations they lead.

The Desert

"The Lord's anger burned against Israel and he made them wonder in the desert forty years, until the whole generation of those who had done evil in his sight was gone" (Numbers 32:13, NIV).

5

The Devil in Sheep's Clothing

"Watch out for false prophets. They come to you in sheep's clothing, but inwardly they are ferocious wolves. By their fruits you will recognize them...For I hear the slander of many; there is terror on every side; they conspire against me and plot to take my life. But I trust in you, O Lord...My times are in your hands; deliver me from my enemies...Let me not be put to shame, O Lord...but let the wicked be put to shame...let their lying lips be silenced"...(Matthew 7: 15-16; Psalm 31: 13, 15, 17-18; NIV).

As soon as I accepted the appointment at Tiny Town, I began receiving phone calls from Pastor Kim, the outgoing pastor, Jodie, her "administrative assistant", and Crystal, the current Lay Leader. I was clued in by Pastor Kim that there were problems at the church and some were severe enough to cause her to be moved to another congregation at the other end of the state. However, I was not told how severe the problems were, and I would not find that out immediately, either. I would learn this over time.

All of their many, many conversations with me for the two months prior to my arrival there sent red flags flying. I sensed there might be some problems there but no one, including Adam or Alyce had warned me that this church was the church that no one else would pastor!

The week before we moved was a bit nerve-wracking, to say the least. My head was spinning from the steady flow of e-mails and phone calls from Pastor Kim, Jodie, and Crystal about the church at Tiny Town. In spite of all of this, I believed God called me there and I spent the entire week in constant prayer about our move.

We sold our home and we packed what we were taking with us to our new ministry location. The rest of our belongings went to storage. On moving day, we loaded the truck, both cars and our small utility trailer. When we pulled out of our driveway, we said goodbye to our family heritage, our home church, and all of our family and friends, and headed for Small Town, America. Several hours after we left home, we arrived in that very small and deserted ghost town. When we drove into town, the first thing that we noticed was the town sign, population 350! But, there was no town. We passed two closed down night-spots and a closed café. We did notice a relatively new school—elementary, middle and high school all in one spot—and the Methodist church close by. As we drove around our new community, we noticed a small general store, a quickie gas station, two churches, and a few scattered small independent businesses. No doubt, this was the smallest town I had ever seen.

I arrived at Tiny Town Church one June day, expecting to have a truly wonderfully spirit-filled ministry as I had had in the past. I just figured that we would love these folks so much that the problems would just go away. Only one person in my past didn't like me, I reasoned, and that was Larry; but since we left Larry behind, I figured all of that drama would be left behind too.

When we made the turn onto "Church" Street, we spotted the beautiful old buildings of the church resting peacefully in the quiet neighborhood. The architecture of the building reminded me of all of the old Methodist churches built in that period, so I felt right at home. We pulled into the church yard and were instantly met by several of the church men who began unloading the truck and placing our belongings into our new home. I was welcomed by several of the Ladies of the church who began to help me unpack the vehicles and small trailer. Everyone seemed so happy that we were there.

Jodie was the first lady to meet me at the car. She immediately began unloading my vehicle and trailer, which I thought was extremely nice. Our new home was a maze of confusion, boxes, furniture, and new faces all trying to help to squeeze three-thousand square feet of furniture into one-thousand square feet of living space. Everyone was friendly, welcoming and eager to help us get settled in as their new pastoral family. Little did I know that soon we would be betrayed by one or more of these helpful "saints"!

As I would soon discover, there were many in the congregation who were mourning the loss of their pastor. As I would also soon discover, there were more who were glad to see her go and who welcomed someone new and fresh. But because I was so happy to be at Tiny Town Church, I did not realize that, instead of lessening their sense of loss, my arrival had deepened it in some ways, since the presence of a new pastor was the surest reminder that the old one was really gone and change was happening no matter what!

This move would be a different experience for our family, too. Our new home was extremely close to the church. As you can imagine, privacy would be limited and my office hours would be 24/7, unless I managed to take my two days off each week and escape to the farm with my husband. Our living arrangements were classified as "sub-standard" by the Methodist Church, and I have to agree with them. But, our family was sent to this place by God to serve His people, regardless of our "standards". I was happy to be their pastor and we were all anxious to get settled in our new home, church and district.

By this time, I understood some of the dynamics of our new ministry setting. First of all, I understood that Pastor Kim, Jodie, and Alyce shared a very close friendship, the level of which Jodie would reveal to me at our first meeting in the days ahead; and Secondly, I understood that this was a hurting congregation, the severity of which I would learn over time. I had no idea actually what was ahead!

I made it through the first Sunday's services with ease. We had a record crowd in attendance and everyone greeted us with excitement. The entire congregation seemed very happy we were there.

Instead of hosting a reception for the new pastoral family as was written protocol of the district, the leaders of the church had other plans for our first Sunday. I found myself in my first church council meeting. While I thought that a bit odd, and wondered what was so urgent that this meeting could not have waited until I had been able to unpack and move into the pastor's church office, I sat quietly and listened and expressed how happy I was to be their new pastor. As I sat patiently, and listened intently, I was deciding what my plan of attack would be. Finally, I decided to spend the first few months of my new appointment observing the workings of the congregation in the church and refrain from making changes. My focus was mainly going to be observation and concentrating on Spirit-filled worship and providing a worship experience that would enable the Holy Spirit to come alive within each worshiper.

I worked diligently at getting a schedule planned so I would be more organized. After all, this was my first full-time appointment. As a part-time pastor, my primary responsibility was to show up for worship on Sunday and preach. This was different and no one had offered any help in outlining what was expected of me as a new full-time pastor. So, I began my ministry at Tiny Town somewhat at a loss! Problems wasted no time in getting started and immediately I encountered power struggles between six individuals that caused me great concern. Each person claimed to be the boss and each one had their own agenda. I had no mentor and I was afraid of my new supervisor, Alyce, because of his relationship with and strong support of the previous pastor, Pastor Kim, and their mutual friend, Jodie. To this day, I do not know or understand why I was intimidated by this man. Fear is a strange thing!

Day by day, I did what most clergy do. I answered the telephone, sent out letters and bulletins to members not in Sunday worship that week, prepared for the following week's worship, obtained and reviewed all mail received, visited the sick and made "Meet Your Pastor" visits to get to know the membership. I learned that when I looked around for clergy support, I was the only person there. I had become the one that most of the church members called when they landed in the emergency room or were having surgery, or just needed their pastor to provide comfort. And, I was the one who got the blame for everything that was wrong with the church. In the early days, I was clued in to this by listening how Jodie verbally crucified her dear friend, Pastor Kim. My time was just around the corner.

During my first few months at Tiny Town, I talked to scores of people suffering from addiction, eviction, physical abuse, bankruptcy, multiple personality disorder, and depression. I not only learned that my new job involved caring for people who were not on the membership rolls, but I also learned that Small Town, America, had a dark side that I had not seen from the front steps of Tiny Town Church. There may not have been homeless people sleeping at the fellowship hall door, but we were in the middle of the poorest of the poor; where making, using, and selling drugs were the norms, and where stealing other people's property was their main occupation! These folks thought nothing of stealing from the church, the pastor, or each other.

The water began to boil that very first week! On Wednesday evening of that week, the church treasurer, Bertha, approached me and told me that I was not to open any of the mail…that I had no right to know what bills were received or any of the information on the bank statements. As a matter of fact, I was not to know anything about the financial situation of the church. I kindly and lovingly informed her that the pastor of the church is supposed to clearly understand all aspects of the church's condition including, but not limited to, it's financial condition. She refused to accept this answer and told me that Diane would not approve of this! I was told before I arrived that Diane was the main "boss" of the church. She previously was the finance chair and now held one of the highest lay positions, and she apparently had everyone in the church believing she ran the church. She probably did, too! The entire church was afraid to cross her because she was the largest money person of the church and she had threatened to leave and take her money with her. The folks at Tiny Town Church feared that they would not be able to survive as a church if Diane left and took her money, so they tried to keep her happy at all costs.

I was further told by Bertha, and confirmed by Jodie, that since I was not Pastor Kim, the previous pastor, they were not going to get along with me. That this "arrangement" was not going to work! Bertha said she did not have to like me or work with me and that she would just wait a few months and I'd be gone and they would get someone else that she could work with. Jodie said that if I did not do what she said to do, I would "be sorry" because she always got her way and if she didn't, she would "get even".

I tried to diffuse this situation by telling both of these ladies that, while I was not Pastor Kim, I was sure we could get along with each other. I did say that I insisted on following our church's rules for doing business and running the church. I lovingly and patiently explained to these ladies that I was neutral in all disputes, that I did not play favorites or take sides or form alliances...that I was their pastor, their Spiritual leader, and I was there to lead them through the appropriate way the Methodist Church does church, hopefully bringing peaceful resolutions to their attitudes of fear and discontent that I sensed were beginning to build.

I made a stand that day for **the Book of Discipline of the UMC**, which outlines the pastor's responsibilities. I pointed out that the pastor has the ultimate responsibility for the church. They needed to understand that Tiny Town UMC did not "belong" to them—they did not own it—it belonged to the greater United Methodist Church—the Conference; and, that the pastor was the "CEO" of the church and had the responsibility to make sure it worked properly and effectively.

For a church who has never understood this concept, this was going to be a difficult task. For a church that had never followed the rules of the church, teaching and enforcing proper procedures for handling the church's business was going to be nearly impossible. As a result, I spent most of the early months there battling ungodly behaviors that were aimed at destroying character, ministry, faith and God's spirit. I have never in my life encountered such behavior in a congregation.

In **Leaving Church**[14], Barbara Brown Taylor talks about transference of emotions and feelings, where human beings sometimes transfer the feelings they have, for or against, one pivotal person in their lives to another pivotal person in their lives, especially when they are feeling vulnerable in a relationship. I began to think about this and to understand that much of the negativity was being directed toward me when it was really directed toward their previous pastor, Kim. They felt abandoned by Kim, even though her leaving was not her decision. They were, therefore, angry at me because I was not Kim. I reminded them of someone else who was no longer around but who had made such an impact on their lives, both positively and negatively, that they were still trying to figure things out. They wanted me to be Kim

---

[14] *Leaving Church*, Barbara Brown Taylor; HarperOne, HarperCollins Publishers; Page 73; New York, New York; 2006.

so that things would not change. I was thankful, though, that God provided a wonderful group of angels who gathered around me and supported me throughout this ordeal. I praise God for them each and every day.

It was obvious that most of the folks of Tiny Town Church were lacking a good solid spiritual foundation in their lives. I was tuned in to this when I opened the door to the Sanctuary late one Saturday evening and found Vacation Bible School decorations adorning every area of the worship area. There was a huge stuffed octopus sitting on the altar table and perched in the middle of the open Bible. There were fish hanging over the pulpit and fish nets and other sea creatures scattered all around our sanctuary; there was even a huge fish net in the choir loft with a huge fish hanging down in the middle of it, all of which covered the lighting to the entire stage area. I immediately wondered what Jesus would have said and done if he had walked into that same situation.

I wondered how difficult it was going to be to bring this congregation into a worshipful atmosphere and feeling in this beach and fishing environment. I tried to overlook the sea creature motif as I placed the octopus and the other sea life adorning the altar table and pulpit, on the floor in a semi-circle in front of them, but one could tell that those responsible were distraught as they entered the sanctuary for worship the next morning.

These actions displayed a lack of respect for our worship area and a lack of respect for their new pastor by not keeping the pastor informed of their intentions. While I did not object to decorations that were spiritual and season appropriate, I did object to turning our worship space into an underwater sea adventure. My point is this: these folks could have decorated the fellowship hall and all of the Sunday school rooms entirely, but they should have respected the worship environment and should have discussed their thoughts for crossing this boundary with the pastor. This respect for God, their pastor and the worship space was absent from Tiny Town Church.

As a solution to these issues, I tried to give them more grown-up ways of conceiving of God, but few were interested in that. They were totally engaged in the drama and gossip that had plagued that church for decades prior to my arrival. No one was following the rules of the church. Rather, it was the plan of the week around there and this appeared to have been going on for many, many, years. Each of the "Seven" had their own agenda's and was leading in their own directions. What I soon found out was that it was almost impossible for anyone to come in to that church and run the church the way the Methodist Church said to run it. It was virtually impossible to do church according to the church rules.

Over time, I became so busy trying to put out fires and keep the peace that I had neglected the one who had called me there. God called me into His ministry. Those He calls, He equips for the task. God equipped me to be an advocate for Him and for the Bible and for "right worship": to do things right. When I answered the call into ministry, I made the commitment to God to strive for His identity, to strive for the identity of God; to do things according to His Word, first and foremost, and secondly to do things according to the rules of the church I had pledged to serve.

Honestly, I shouldn't have expected this church to be any different…all of the leadership was flawed. The clergy leadership performed like rock stars on stage complete with head-set mics and shiny shark-skin suits; and the leadership team did not follow our rule book, **The Book of Discipline of The United Methodist Church**, in managing clergy, congregants, or the church. When multiple complaints were filed in accordance with the **Book of Discipline**, they were dismissed. The church was out of control; the people involved were spreading vicious gossip about the other church members, the pastor, and their supervising clergy; Alyce was triangulated in a relationship with the previous pastor and Jodie, and became paranoid about all of this gossip and was sure that people were gossiping about him. This was the wildest rodeo I had ever experienced and in all of this chaos, where was the mission and ministry of the church? Had we all forgotten about that?

There was one power struggle after another at Tiny Town. Jodie was the controller who managed to weasel her way onto every committee of the church and basically gained control of the church and all of its programs. She threatened others as well as the pastor if she didn't get on the committees she wanted or in the position she wanted. Cathy was one of the main gossipers who took every complaint she heard for herself or from Jodie, directly to Alyce and tattled her version to him. Jodie and Cathy never followed church protocol by coming to the pastor to discuss issues so the pastor, and every pastor who had served that church before, remained completely in the dark about all of the complaints until an explosion erupted. I knew nothing was being plotted behind my back against me for over six months.

Then, Crystal, the Lay Leader, took great pleasure in releasing her venom toward anyone she thought was opposing her. In one meeting, she was so angered she cursed and screamed and spewed spit at me and others seated around the table. I was told by Jodie that Crystal told one of the members in a meeting that she was like "pus in a boil"! Can you imagine this kind of disgusting language in church?

Bertha, the Church Treasurer, together with Jodie, manipulated the money of the church. They moved money from one account to the other with Jodie directing where it should go. Jodie was not on the finance committee or involved in the inner workings of the church to the point where she had authority to do such a thing so I questioned them both about what I had heard and seen. I also questioned Jodie about going through the deposit slips and viewing the congregation's record of giving, which was listed on them. I had complaints from other members that Jodie was talking outside of church about how much individuals were giving to the church. As a matter of fact, she and Pastor Kim disclosed this information to me prior to my arrival there. These two were furious with me that I would question their actions. I disclosed this to Alyce but he dismissed this charge. Later, after Crystal openly stated to him that she refused to follow any of the rules for the Treasurer as outlined in the **Book of Discipline,** Alyce told me to replace her. Replacing Crystal started another explosion. She wrote a slanderous letter to the church congregation and sent it out to each member making statements that totally were not true about me, their pastor, and that could be verified as not true. In addition to all of these power plays, the congregation attempted to claim ownership of the pastor as well.

Among the first, and there were many that surfaced in those first few weeks, problems I encountered centered on friendships and alliances. Soon after we arrived at Tiny Town, my husband

and I gravitated toward a family close in age with us and who shared the same interests. We enjoyed visiting with them away from the church. Soon another couple joined us, then another. This was not an inclusive group and anyone was free to join us. But mostly, it was just us and one or two couples. What surprised me was the negative gossip that developed and was circulated because the pastor had developed these social relationships outside of the church and church activities.

In a small rural town of three-hundred people, there are few opportunities to develop a social life away from church. It is unreasonable to ask the pastor not to develop friendships within the congregation; as long as the pastor-parish boundaries are maintained. These boundaries were present and this was understood without ever having a discussion on the subject. The Shepherd and the flock gathered for fellowship; all were welcome, but only a few came.

It was nearly impossible to have an uninterrupted worship. These evil doers walked out during worship if they didn't like something that was said; they spread tales about the pastor and other congregants; they attempted and were successful many times to dismantle many of the programs of the church; they pledged to get even, to get rid of, and to disgrace the pastor and those who supported the pastor and the ministries of the church. They stole the pastor's utility trailer containing the pastor's clothes, from the church yard; they staged break-ins into the church; they stalked the pastor at all hours of the night; and they pranked phone called the pastor at all hours of the day and night on the church phone and on the pastor's personal phone. During my year of ministry there, I was emotionally abused and harassed repeatedly. All of this happened while the people of God sat in their pews and did nothing to stand up and fight this evil that was invading God's house.

A reflection was written about the situation by one of the ex-members. It read: *"There was a certain person in the 'church' who used his position to carry on a close personal relationship with a female pastor. He himself was also a pastor. This inappropriate relationship had the direct effect of completely destroying a whole church congregation. The fall out of this relationship went all the way to the top and was ultimately covered up and dismissed. Even the leaders at the top would not address this situation with these two pastors and these two were triangulated with a small gossip group within the church. The situation was horrible and it was all covered up and no one who deserved justice got to see any of it. There was no healing for anyone; everyone was a loser in all of this. It was totally senseless. The two pastors involved are still in their positions in the church. The chances of this cycle of events occurring again, without any discussion and no accountability on the part of these individuals, are very good. They are still out there and who will they offend next?...It seems that those in authority simply do not care about the people that they are serving, they only care about themselves...Many struggle in the falsehood of their pseudo religious system; they are playing a game of trying to pick good fruit off of bad trees, pretending to apply what they consider to be the truth, and reaping rotten fruit in a never ending cycle!...This all sounds like a soap opera, where everyone has their own agenda and their own version of the truth. It seems impossible that these circumstances can exist in a church, but they do!"*[15]

---

[15] These statements were taken from a reflection paper written by an ex-member for a class on **Preventing Sexual Abuse in Congregations;** Ex-member of Tiny Town Church wishes to remain anonymous; 2013. Used with written permission.

I knew that this was the work of Satan—of Evil; and that each of these evil-doers was a devil in sheep's clothing disguised to deceive God's people...but why? And who was the ring leader? Who kept the gossip train running? Was Satan really working in our church? I never would have admitted that this was a possibility if I had not read a riveting book by Rebecca Nichols Alonzo titled **The Devil in Pew Number Seven**[16] just a few weeks prior. Actually, I only read a chapter or two and put this book down because I found it so hard to believe. A few weeks or so after leaving the ministry at Tiny Town, I picked this book up again and finished it. It was amazing to see what extremes Satan goes to in order to destroy Christ's servants. I have found that Satan wants to destroy us, that's a fact. Satan is in our worship meetings, disguised as innocent sweet people, and sits beside us as we sing our songs and lift our hearts in praise. In Rebecca's book, the devil in her story always sat in pew number seven. In my story, oddly enough, one of the devils sat in pew number seven too! I found that quite amazing!

Looking back at Tiny Town, and based on all of the evidence I have collected, this is what I believed happened: Alyce had a close friendship with the previous pastor (Kim), whom I was replacing. Kim and her close friend and congregant, Jodie, stressed this close relationship with Alyce many times. So, right off I knew that there was some sort of close friendship between these three that affected the congregation and its leadership. Because of the relationship between them, I was intimidated and afraid to discuss this with Alyce. Then, pulled into this three-some were: Diane,

---

[16] Alonzo, Rebecca Nichols; **The Devil in Pew Number Seven;** 2010; Tyndale Momentum, An imprint of Tyndale House Publishers, Inc.; Carol Stream, IL.

the leader; Bertha, the Treasurer; Cathy, the gossip; Crystal, the Lay Leader; and Dusty, the enabler. I later found out that Jodie was the glue that held this den of vipers together.

Kim left and went to the other end of the state to a new church position. Alyce was angry at the church for having Kim moved, and he was angry at me because I was not Kim and didn't play by her agenda. Suddenly, the dynamics drastically changed. Jodie was the next to leave. She could not just be a worshipper. She had to be in control of everything. When she lost control, she left the church. But the sad thing was that she and the others that did not leave the church, made up lies about their pastor, and others, and spread them throughout the community and to Alyce.

From the lies he received, Alyce perceived me to be something I absolutely was not. However, a person's perception of situations or actions becomes their truth. He perceived me to be a threat, arrogant, unreachable, un-leadable, a bad leader of others, a poor manager, and a gossip, among other things[17]. Never once did he attempt to get to know me, or teach me, or lead me, or to even discuss his perceptions of me, with me. And, because of his perceptions and his insecurities, he turned his feelings and perceptions into fact. These perceptions were based on lies and gossip constantly fed to him from this gossip group who were in his inner circle. Never once did he insist that these members take their issues to the pastor or through the proper channels in the local church, as the rules state. Rather, he made the decision to bypass these rules and act on these issues as if they were true and as if he had the authority to do so. But why? What was his

---

[17] Information taken from personal letter I received from Adam

motive for doing this? Well, Alyce, knowing he had secrets to keep hidden, was afraid that he would be exposed like Larry was (remember Larry from Chapters 1 and 2?) You see, Alyce knew I knew Larry from my home church. He assumed that I was responsible for Larry's arrest for his bad behaviors. All of the clergy leadership were ordered to keep Larry's pending situation quiet. And, Adam did not want this present situation to be made public any more than it already was. Alyce was afraid that I would 'expose' him and his "secrets", whatever they were.

What he did next was unthinkable; it was un-Christian, unbiblical, and definitely against all laws and rules of the Church. Alyce took his misinformation, lies, perceptions, and whatever else you want to call them, without discussing his thoughts with the church or Pastor-Parish Relations Committee or Pastor, to Adam, and in a real panic mode, preached his version of the truth in order to convince Adam that I should no longer be a minister there[18].

In spite of all of this gossip and nonsense that was being spread about the church and their new pastor, attendance and offerings were at an all-time high. People who had not come to church for a long time, were now beginning to attend. The church was beginning to grow again. But, the more we did and the stronger and more active the Holy Spirit became, the harder this group of seven tried to destroy it. When they could not achieve this, they aimed at my ministry.

I guess the goal of these evil doers—Satan's Seven— was to destroy the leader and the rest would crumble. So, this became

---

[18] Information concerning the meeting was obtained from a source who wishes to remain anonymous

the focus of this group. Our church was at its peak. It was amazing how excited about God everyone was. I never saw a church come back from the brink of disaster so fast as this one did in those eleven months.

Then, one evening, totally unaware that anything major was brewing, Alyce appeared in my office and, breaking every rule of our church, and without giving any reason, fired me from my position as pastor, which, I found out later, he had no authority to do. In those few minutes, Alyce attempted to destroy my ministry and that church. He almost succeeded too. Because of his actions, I had to move to another state in order to practice ministry. Most of the congregation who were God's warriors, left too. Tiny Town Church was in ruins.

Satan works with all his might to destroy God's servants. I would never have thought that these types of things could ever happen in the church. The church is supposed to be a happy place filled with peace and love—a safe place. But, I have learned that where there is goodness, evil lurks nearby to attempt to destroy it. Matthew 17 warns us about the devil in sheep's clothing, and we are warned throughout the Scripture about the "evil ones".

"Be self-controlled and alert. Your enemy the devil prowls around like a roaring lion looking for someone to devour. Resist him, standing firm in the faith..." (1 Peter 5:8-9; NIV). These devils work for Satan to achieve his goals. They are real. I know. I have met them!

Amid all of the suffering and chaos, I knew that I had to make a change. I felt that God was calling me to leave this place. But sometimes, a call like this is hard to accept. I had never experienced anything quite like this and it was extremely painful. Still, I hung on, thinking that maybe I was wrong; that God wanted me to stay and try harder to bring peace to this church in crisis. I was struggling with God much like we read about in the Scriptures. But for me, God said it was time to go. And He took control in a way that I did not understand and found hard to reckon with; but with a huge reward waiting on the other side of it all.

What I learned from this experience was that people who continue to neglect their relationship with God—those who battle for control and power—just plain forget their creator and the whole point of being alive! Their problems are truly Spiritual problems of the greatest proportions. Our churches are in trouble!

"Blessed are you when people insult you, persecute you and falsely say all kinds of evil against you because of me. Rejoice and be glad, because great is your reward in heaven, for in the same way they persecuted the prophets who were before you". (Matthew 5: 11-12). In the days ahead, I would utter these words many times.

6

Politics in the Church?

"But he who received seed on the good ground is he who hears the word and understands it, who indeed bears fruit and produces: some a hundredfold, some sixty, some thirty...he who sows the good seed is the Son of Man (God)...the good seeds are the sons of the kingdom (you and me) "(Matthew13: 23, 37, 38 KJV).

In all of my years as a church member, I never imagined the church as being political. To me, politics and God just don't exactly go together. However, as a pastor in the Methodist church for several years, I was able to see the church through a different lens.

I was born and raised in a large Methodist Church during the late forties to mid-sixties. While I am sure there were problems, the problems we encountered mostly had to deal with disagreements as a result of differences in personal theologies.

The pastors were rarely educated beyond the bachelor level, if that far, and there was absolutely no doubt that these godly preachers were filled with the Holy Spirit and that the Holy Spirit flowed throughout the entire worship experience. We had a very special respect for our pastors because they were helping us understand God's gifts and graces and promises…they were, in essence, God's representatives to us, His people. Yes, church and ministry was very different back then.

As I remember, our district superintendents would come to our church for special church meetings and worship and we were blessed by these special events. We felt honored to have them with us. We had an enormous amount of respect for our pastors and our district superintendents and their love and ministry to us left us with no doubt that they were Godly servants. This type of respect is rarely seen in the church today. In my ministry, I have experienced two district superintendents that left no doubt in my mind that the Holy Spirit was leading them in their ministries. They are truly wonderful leaders whom I hold in the highest regard.

I am sad to say that some of our clergy and clergy leadership act like theatrical performers when they are in front of a crowd. After all, they are human with their own human, earthly agenda's. Sometimes these personal agenda's may be different from God's agenda and their leadership reflects this. This calls into question things like calling, agenda, Holy Spirit, Filling, and Works of Flesh. We have discussed calling and agenda already. I will discuss the action of the Holy Spirit, Filling with the Holy Spirit and Works of the Flesh in future chapters.

When I entered seminary I developed a richer and deeper spiritual life. I looked at everything differently. As a result, I began to see that there were people entering the ministry as a profession—a vocation—rather than a way of life and a truly spiritual venture as God's representative to His people. They looked upon the ministry as a job with a good salary and benefits. Oddly enough most of these folks were the younger males who were new college graduates just entering seminary—the typical seminarians—and preparing for their lives ahead. They were inexperienced and immature in their view of ministry. Naturally, they were motivated with things of the "world" like money, power, prestige, and climbing that corporate ladder. They wanted to someday become a district superintendent and maybe even a bishop. Very few of my new colleagues viewed ministry from the first century servant aspect of the true Jesus followers.

My journey into ministry was long and often disappointing. I felt that many of the difficulties I encountered were due to the fact that I was an older, second vocation woman, instead of the typical young male that the church so fervently solicits for their clergy. I tended to view ministry, the congregation and the church through the lens of Godly maturity, a quality that was the result of spiritual maturation and life experiences. As a matter of fact, my seminary classes contained more seasoned second career students and pastors than the typical and longed-for younger males. We, the seasoned second career pastors, are often patronized and looked down on and placed in problem churches that no one else wants. We are made to feel second rate or not as good as our younger colleague. When we encounter those who have their own agenda's, those who are controlling and judgmental, we are often misunderstood and may appear threatening. Our ministries are often called into question.

I encountered these forms of politics personally and it eventually led to a huge political battle for control in our church. The Methodist Church does have in place a judicial process for solving disputes and other issues concerning clergy and the laity. This process is clearly stated in **The Book of Discipline of The United Methodist Church**, the church's rule book. As clergy, when we become licensed and ordained ministers, we pledge to follow the rules of our denomination as outlined in this book and failure to do so is grounds for formal charges.

Disobedience to the order and discipline of the United Methodist Church refers to disobeying the rules of the church as outlined in its **Book of Discipline**. I am increasingly surprised to learn how many clergy and church leaders have no idea what our rule book says. Almost all denominations have a set of rules that their clergy and church leaders are to follow. Each prospective church member needs to clearly understand what these rules are before they become church members. These denominations and organizations have a statement of faith and core values which outlines what they believe and basically how they do church. Folks who agree to a certain group's guidelines for doing church and worship usually bind together to form their community of faith. If you are going to commit to a certain community, that community expects you to abide by their rules and guidelines. The Methodist Church is no different. Even our little prairie church, has a statement of faith and ministry values so that each congregant knows our philosophy and what they can expect from their pastor.

Most of the breakdown in communicating the responsibilities of new members rest with the pastor accepting these new members into that particular church. The Methodist Church expects each pastor to have membership classes for those who are joining from other denominations so that they will understand how that particular church functions. However, I was made aware that this did not happen at Tiny Town and the previous pastor accepted several new members from other denominations without any membership classes. Tiny Town Church is no different from many others. This technicality gets overlooked in our excitement to welcome newcomers. So, over time, folks begin to think that they can do church however they want—that the church is theirs to run it however they want.

What is the excuse for clergy not knowing how their church functions? This was the core problem of the trouble at Tiny Town. The members and church leaders at Tiny Town had no idea what the **Book of Discipline** said…some didn't even know what the **Book of Discipline** was. The previous pastor was relatively new to the ministry and transferred into the Methodist Church from another denomination. Based on the decisions she made during her ministry at Tiny Town, she was unaware of the contents of this book. Actually, some of her decisions were down right unethical and illegal, according to church policy, rules and regulations. For instance, she baptized minor children of unchurched families without the proper consent, she failed to keep accurate attendance and membership records as required by the church, and she failed to report the accurate figures on the proper Charge Conference reports at the end of the church year. These reports reflect how that particular church is doing in regards to programs started, attendance gained or lost, among other things. In other words, a bad report or one that shows low activity, income, attendance and membership would alert the upper management that the pastor is not doing his/her job at that church. These are the signs and symptoms of a dying church. If a pastor wants to be recognized for his/her achievements in order to move up the corporate church ladder, then they certainly do not want anyone to know that their current church is failing.

Because of her inability to lead and manage, she could not teach the church how to do church according to the church rules. This led to confusion, mistrust, personal agendas, gossip rings, ownership power plays, and ultimately to a fractured and dysfunctional congregation.

Some clergy believe that the church system is flawed and fractured. Some even say it is failing and the reason, according to **Good News Magazine,** is this: "*...many of our bishops are unwilling to enforce the* **Book of Discipline** *and the covenant we have agreed to live by...disregard of that covenant...demonstrates the deep division and conflicting worldviews existing within The United Methodist Church"*[19].

This article is primarily referring to the same-sex marriage issue. However, the same-sex marriage issue is only one of the problems facing the church today. It is not just about this issue and whether or not clergy should perform these unions. It is about supporting the rules and regulations that the Methodist Church, and any church, stands for and those that we as clergy pledge to support. Some clergy leadership think nothing about interpreting laws of the church however they wish in order to achieve their agenda.

There were two people in a position to correct the problems at Tiny Town: Adam and Alyce. Here is where politics came into play. Alyce developed a close personal friendship with the Pastor Kim. Over time, one congregant, Jodie, also became part of that

---

[19] **Good News Magazine;** http://goodnewsmag.org/; *"Good News finds present UM situation untenable";* April 2, 2014.

inner circle and together, they made most of the decisions for the Tiny Town church. They excluded the other members, except for four others. When the congregation decided to take their church back, major problems erupted and there was an all-out campaign to get rid of Pastor Kim. Alyce became angry at the church because he was forced to move Pastor Kim to another church. Because of this, he lost his credibility with the congregation as a spiritual leader. His anger interfered with his ability to supervise this church and the new pastor objectively. Then the old career ladder syndrome took center stage: *"Frankly, fellow clergy are hard to live with. The nature of the 'career ladder' for pastoral moves, and a highly limited number of prime appointments makes us all competitors with one another more than colleagues in loving covenant. 'Worldly' is very much a word that describes The United Methodist Church.*[20]".

When I arrived at Tiny Town as the new pastor, nothing I did was right. These six congregants and members of Alyce's inner circle went to him with every issue they had. Alyce could have followed the **Book of Discipline** and referred these congregants back to the pastor or Pastor-Parish Relations Committee, whose job it was to handle issues concerning the pastor. However, he chose not to do this. Instead, he chose to bypass all of the rules of the **Book of Discipline** concerning procedures for handling issues in the local church, and to step outside of his role as God's representative, and to assume his own agenda for his own personal gain.

When my ministry at Tiny Town ended, the pastoral relations committee and its Chairman, the Church Council and many

---

[20] www.thoughtfulpastor.com; *"Called and Gifted"*; April 24, 2013.

others in the congregation wrote letters to Adam on my behalf telling him how Alyce had treated this church and its pastor. The church was in ruins. So many lives had been destroyed and their spiritual foundations left crumbling. Many had lost faith in the Methodist Church.

The church needed to see its leadership following the guidelines in their book of rules. They needed to see that this is what we do as United Methodists; this is how we make our church run the way it was designed to run. My sheep needed to see that goodness steps forward and does what it can to stop and control evil, because goodness will not let evil run rampant! The members pulled together in a last ditch effort to save their church and their pastor who had been terminated against the church's wishes. Nothing seemed to make any difference.

This sequence of events reminds me of the parable of *"The Sower"* in Matthew 13 as mentioned at the beginning of this chapter. Jesus told a parable about a farmer who went out to sow seed. As he was scattering the seed, some fell along the path, and the birds came and ate it up. Some fell on rocky places, where it did not have much soil. It sprang up quickly, because the soil was shallow. But when the sun came up, the plants were scorched, and they withered because they had no root.

Other seed fell among thorns, which grew up and choked the plants. Still other seed fell on good soil, said Jesus, where it produced a crop--a hundred, sixty or thirty times what was sown.

Jesus' disciples asked him to explain this parable. Jesus replied, "When anyone hears the message about the kingdom and does not understand it, the evil one comes and snatches away what was sown in his heart. This is the seed sown along the path.

The one who received the seed that fell on rocky places is the man who hears the Word and at once receives it with joy. But since he has no root, he lasts only a short time. When trouble or persecution comes because of the Word, he quickly falls away.

The one who received the seed that fell among the thorns is the man who hears the word, but the worries of this life and the deceitfulness of wealth choke it, making it unfruitful. But the one who received the seed that fell on good soil is the man who hears the word and understands it. He produces a crop, yielding a hundred, sixty or thirty times what was sown."

Now there are some things that are evident in this parable. The farmer is God. And the seed is the message of the Kingdom. I want to focus on the good soil that yields a hundred, sixty or thirty times what was sown, because that good soil is you and me. We are those who have received the message of the kingdom and have said yes to it. Now, what kind of crop are we producing? What kind of crop do we see is being produced in our churches? Because we are co-laborers with God, it is now our turn to sow seed. What seed are we sowing?

You don't have to be someone special to sow seeds of the kingdom. You don't have to be a superstar. You don't have to be a celebrity. One of the surest teachings of scripture is that anybody can be used of God to do the work of the kingdom.

Few of the heroes of the Bible, particularly the Old Testament, are heroic at all. They did some really stupid things, just like you and just like me. But God still used them, just as God can use us. You don't have to be someone special to sow seeds of the kingdom.

However, you do need to be committed. This is the most important secret in life: You and I can accomplish extraordinary things if we are willing to pay the price; the price of commitment: living for Christ.

How do we become a sower of seed? You don't have to be someone special to sow seeds of the kingdom, but you do need to be committed. You do have to know what you believe and you have to give yourself completely to that belief. You need to be committed to living for Jesus. You do need to be committed to living in the Word and not of the world. To make a difference in the world requires a high level of commitment. And this can be achieved if we're willing to pay the price. That is why a cross stands at the center of our worship. Someone was willing to pay the price for us.

People often ask, was it necessary for Christ to die upon the cross? Obviously it was. We, of course, cannot see into the mind of God, but Christ dying on a cross is a reminder to us that if our lives are to have any impact on our world, we are going to have to give our lives to something bigger than ourselves. Humanity never moves forward unless someone is willing to go beyond the efforts of the ordinary or the average. God was committed to saving humanity from its own foolish ways. How do we know? It is because of the cross. We will never be able to save our failing church communities unless we take a stand for Christ and His Church.

So, I ask you what kind of seed are you sowing in the lives of those you love? In the community? In the world for which Christ died? In the church? What kind of seeds did Larry, Adam, Alyce, and 'Satan's Seven' sow?

Will this be a better world because you've been here? It doesn't take a lot of talent to make a difference in the world. All it takes is someone willing to take up a cross.

7

Making Sense of it All

"To keep me from becoming conceited because of these surpassingly great revelations, there was given me a thorn in my flesh, a messenger of Satan, to torment me. Three times I pleaded with the Lord to take it away from me. But he said to me, 'My grace is sufficient for you, for my power is made perfect in weakness.' Therefore I will boast all the more gladly about my weaknesses, so that Christ's power may rest on me. That is why, for Christ's sake, I delight in weaknesses, in insults, in hardships, in persecutions, in difficulties. For when I am weak, then I am strong" (2 Corinthians 12: 7-10, NIV).

No matter what situations we find ourselves enmeshed in, we must have the faith to realize that God, first of all, never gives us more than we can bear. And secondly, we must have the faith to realize that God puts us in situations for our benefit and growth, even though these situations may sometimes be unpleasant. Our Lord knows what we need in our lives to grow and mature in our faith. After all, this life is but a training ground for our lives to come!

I have written and re-written this chapter about three times before this final time, trying to find just the right words to share. At first, I was writing more from selfish motives; but now, after several years of healing and many hours of prayer, I write this chapter in an effort to make sense of the events that transpired at Tiny Town and to prepare us all for that healing process. At some time or other, we all may experience our Tiny Town's and we must understand the problems and how to move forward through them.

Everyone involved in this story, including myself, could have done things differently. I will be the first to admit that I was put in a situation that I was unprepared for and instead of seeking out the help I needed from sources outside of my local congregation, I chose to deal with things myself. Maybe I let ego get in the way of right decisions. I am not really sure, but I do know that our Scriptures are clear that there are false teacher, preachers and lay persons in our churches and that all of these persons who move by their own agendas instead of God's, must be held accountable for their actions. The situation at Tiny Town was no different. The shepherd always takes care of his/her sheep; and, my sheep needed to see that their shepherd was leading them according to the laws of God and the church.

Alyce continually, and with all of his might, attempted to undermine my ministry and the ministry of the Tiny Town Church. How he achieved this was un-Christian, un-Biblical, and against the rules of the Methodist Church and its **Book of Discipline**[21].

---

[21] Summary of facts obtained from personal interview of a retired United Methodist Minister who wishes to remain anonymous. Used by written permission.

Long after I had left Tiny Town and was blessed with a new ministry, I received a letter from Adam. I was humbled to know that he understood that the problems at Tiny Town Church existed long before my arrival and, as a matter of fact, had gone on for many years. Adam knew that the church had the symptoms of a dysfunctional congregation, with many of its members moving by their own agendas. I think he also knew that these agendas were being fueled by innuendo, gossip, power-plays and manipulation. In a way, I was relieved to know that Adam also felt that my appointment at Tiny Town was never given a proper chance to succeed because all of these problems were already in place before I got there.

Alyce had acted in a way that was totally unacceptable according the church's rules. What was the reason that Alyce disliked me from the beginning? Why did he want me gone? If he didn't like me, or couldn't work with me, he could have just moved me to another district like he did Pastor Kim. Why did he want me out of the state?

Remember Pastor Larry from earlier chapters? Larry blamed me for his lot in life. I had nothing to do with his problems and behaviors. However, Larry needed someone to blame so he told his friend, Billy, his DS, that I caused his problems at our church. Billy made a note about Larry's accusations and these notes ended up in my ministry file. This file moves around the conference, from district to district, each time the pastor moves. So, when I moved into Alyce's district, the first thing Alyce did was to read my file. In his mind now he's on alert. He became a little worried because he knew that he had not followed the **Book of Discipline** in his leadership of Tiny Town and Pastor Kim and his close friendship with her had rendered him unable to remain objective in his views of that church. He became very defensive and he perceived me as a threat! His perceptions were compounded by lies and gossip told to him by *Satan's Seven* (Tiny Town's gossip group). In his mind, I was the enemy and he had to get rid of me before he ended up exposed like Larry! He then put this big plan in motion and used his gossip group from the church to help him achieve his goal.

This entire thing was a cover up—a plan aimed at saving Alyce's job and not causing embarrassment to the church. This was politics in the church at the highest level! Of course, this is my perception, but be assured that it does exist and we need to clearly understand that it is real. May God have mercy on those who attempt to destroy God's ministers, their ministry, and their congregations.

"For the time will come when men will not put up with sound doctrine. Instead, to suit their own desires, they will gather around them a great number of teachers to say what their itching ears want to hear. They will turn their ears away from the truth and turn aside to myths. But you, keep your head in all situations; endure hardship, do the work of an evangelist, and discharge all the duties of your ministry" (2 Timothy 4:3-5, NIV).

8

Holding the Church Hostage
Understanding the Problems at Tiny Town

"Remind the people to be subject to rulers and authorities, to be obedient, to be ready to do whatever is good, to slander no one, to be peaceable and considerate, and to show true humility toward all men" (Titus 3:1-2, NIV).

Holding a church hostage? What a horrible thought! About a year ago, I read an article that was posted on Facebook with this same title. The article was written by Dayton L. Owen[22], and its focus has remained with me throughout these last few years as I journeyed through ministry. I think it is worth discussing because our small membership churches across this country are in trouble and are failing. Many of the reasons, but not all, can be attributed to those mentioned in this article by Owen. Indeed, many of the problems at the Tiny Town Church were directly related to several of its members who claimed ownership of the

---

[22] http://ministrymatters.com/all/article/author/dyton-1-owen

church and, through this feeling of ownership, did, indeed, hold this church hostage!

Everyone has experienced someone in their church who may have issued ultimatums to the pastor or the Administrative Board with the alternative being that if they did not get their way, they would leave the church. I have experienced folks like this in some of the congregations I have pastored. It is a natural temptation for some to develop feelings of closeness or ownership of a church that has been in their families for generations. They feel that the church is "theirs" without considering that it is actually God's and is only one small part of the whole of God's body of believers. Sadly, it is not always congregants who hold the church hostage. I experienced a clergy who issued ultimatums from the pulpit many times saying, among other things: "…you'd better be glad I'm here; no one else would take this church…" At Tiny Town Church, Jodie told me: "If I don't get what I want, I will get even"; and Cathy told me several times, "We've gotten rid of every pastor we didn't like—we know just how to do that." Not only are these demands extremely hurtful to the congregation and pastor, they are perfect examples of people who have their own agendas and who want either the pastor or the congregation to behave in such a way so as to achieve their goal or else they will release their power over them. This is an example of hostage taking in the church, and if it is left unchallenged, these folks will gain control simply because they make the most noise.

Pastors and congregants must stand firm and address this situation and refuse to let power plays hold their church hostage. The only result of a church held hostage is the loss of ministry and vision that prevents the church from doing the work that it has been called to do.

For the last twenty-five to thirty years, Tiny Town Church, Small Town, America, has been held hostage by six of the church's lay leadership. Through the years there were additions to their little group of renegades. These members prided themselves with their greatest objective: getting rid of the pastors who represented change because they could not control them or whom they just plain did not like. This little group of powerful mouths could conjure up a pot of gossip quicker than instant grits and circulate it throughout the local church and the local community with the zest and zeal of Paul Revere's ride! Their main objective was to obtain power and control, no matter the cost. Sadly, this type of behavior can exist without these folks even being aware that this is what they are doing.

This behavior is not all that uncommon in the small membership church. You see, members whose parents and/or grandparents were charter or founding members, or those with longstanding memberships or histories of bountiful giving, tend to claim ownership of the church. What evolves are power struggles, gossip rings, the inability to change and grow, and the inability to understand and cherish the mission and vision of the church.

Let's take this a step further. In the same manner as we mentioned above, clergy leadership can also hold the local church hostage for a number of reasons, initially, but result in power and control to achieve their goal. In this same small rural church, the dynamics changed considerably when this church received its first female pastor who came with her own agenda and baggage. Trouble always follows when we fail to live and lead by God's agenda. Pastor Kim joined this group of hostage-takers and made the seventh member of the gossip ring, commonly known as "Satan's Seven"!

Over the first half of this new pastor's leadership, she was able to further divide, isolate and enrage the congregation to the level of WWIII; and over the last half of her tour of duty, developed close relationships with her clergy supervisor (Alyce) and one of her congregants, Jodie. These three persons—a clergy, a supervising clergy, and a congregant—became triangulated in a close relationship that essentially held that church hostage through their control tactics which rendered that supervising clergy ineffective in his objective leadership of the congregation and pastor. When the pastor had to be moved to another location, she left behind an impossible situation for the new incoming pastor.

I was this new pastor. Sadness and strife now fill this church. This is the end result of a long history of dysfunction that all started with the small group of members who thought they owned their church. Churches rarely survive dysfunction such as this. In this particular church, a new pastor was brought in to replace the outgoing pastor. Everyone knew, including the supervisors, that this was a deteriorating situation.

The supervising clergy was still caught up in the triangulated relationship with the previous pastor and now ex-congregants. He continued to hold this little church hostage and appeared to rejoice at its failures and denounce its successes. The attendance had steadily declined over the years and dropped 80% overnight when their new pastor left unexpectedly at the hands of the gossip gals and supervising clergy; and at last count, there were 10 people who attended worship that following Sunday morning.

We are divided as a country and this attitude of divisiveness and unwillingness to get along has spilled over into the church. Our Amish friends view church as a body of people not a building, and worship is ALL about God, not us. They remain focused on community and living God-centered lives. They love and support each other at all costs. They do not gossip or participate in activities that are unpleasing to God. Most importantly, they hold their tongues in obedience to God's Word. An Amish proverb says it all: "Blessed are those who have nothing to say and cannot be persuaded to say it"[23]. How different the fate of this small church if this proverb had been lived out over the years!

The problem at Tiny Town Church is truly a spiritual one. In order to prevent this form of behavior from continuing, we must understand more clearly what I perceive the Spiritual problems to be. Those involved in this story have apparently lost their filling of the Holy Spirit, and when one loses his/her filling that person is not yielded to the Spirit. That statement may sound a little hokey or goofy, but it is one that causes great concern for our churches and denominations as we see more and more Christians falling into this category. After this experience, especially, I am more convinced that most folks have a limited understanding of the Holy Spirit and His actions upon our lives. I feel led to move this chapter toward a clearer understanding of this area of our faith. For if we fail to become filled with God's Spirit, then we fail in our Spiritual journey.

The Holy Spirit baptizes the believer, and as Christians, we have learned about the Holy Spirit descending upon the Body of

---

[23] Proverbs 13:3, 15:4 and 25:23

Christ (the twelve Apostles) at Pentecost and filling them. This became one of the most important days of the church because it introduced three completely new elements: The Holy Spirit would now be universal and not limited or confined to Israel, as before (Romans 10:17); The Holy Spirit would now be permanent, which was not the case before Pentecost, because now we are the living temple of God (1 Corinthians 3:16); and the Holy Spirit would be perfecting, to help all repenting Christians grow in grace (2 Corinthians 3: 18; 2 Peter3: 18).

The Holy Spirit baptizes the believer in the Body of Christ to answer Christ's prayer for Christian unity (John 17:21) and to prepare a bride for Christ. That bride is made up of all members of His body composed of all believers saved from the time of Pentecost until the 'Rapture' (Romans 12:5; 1 Corinthians 10: 17, 12:13, 12:27; Ephesians 1: 22-23; Rev. 19:6-9). You see, Spirit baptism places us into the Body of Christ and identifies us with His death (Acts 18:24). Baptism with the Holy Spirit happens only once in a believer's life, it cannot be undone, and it occurs when we believe in Christ. When a person is initially baptized with the Holy Spirit, they are also filled; although they can lose that filling. Filling with the Holy Spirit is an individual experience that can be repeated and it can be lost. It can also occur throughout the Christian life.

I was born into the Methodist denomination and I never learned about the Holy Spirit as a young child. I learned about God and Jesus but I do not ever remember hearing sermons in church on the Holy Spirit and certainly not about being filled with the Spirit. I know that I am not the only person of the Boomer generation and earlier whose denomination and local church failed to properly teach God's Word. It is no wonder that our churches are in trouble today. We were taught that church was a fun place where we went to see our friends and eat big dinners together; where we got to wear our new clothes; and a place where we gathered to go camping together or to go on other fun trips together. But the Holy Spirit? I never learned about the actions of the Holy Spirit until I was an adult preparing for ministry. I am not proud to say this, either. I read about the Holy Spirit in the Scriptures but I knew little about the actions of the Holy Spirit in our lives. When I arrived at Tiny Town Church, I found that I was not the only one who had grown up with limited understanding on the Scriptural teachings about the Holy Spirit. This lacking became more and more evident as the events unfolded.

One of the most amazing things I learned is that there is no pre-requisite to receiving the filling with the Holy Spirit except faith in Christ. You see, continued filling depends on yielded-ness and yielded-ness is continual striving to achieve Christ-like-ness. That is, to act and to treat others as Christ would treat them. It is also to completely yield from the ways of the world and to concern ourselves with things of Christ and to turn from our own selfish agenda's (Romans 8: 9-10; 1 Corinthians 3:16, 6:19; 1 John 4:4; 2 Timothy 1: 14). The Holy Spirit permanently indwells all believers, even in our sin. This is the gift of God for every believer (John 7: 37; Acts 10: 45; Acts 11: 16-17), and the only condition to receive the Holy Spirit is to receive Christ as Savior and Lord!

It is my firm belief that a person who does not have the Holy Spirit within is a lost individual. That is a sad, sad thing to think about. I would rather think that most of the "Seven" were and are believers who have simply lost their way and have fallen out of fellowship with God. A person can leave the fellowship of God but make no mistake about it, the Holy Spirit will never leave that person (Ephesians 4:30). The Holy Spirit seals the believer until the Day of Redemption, according to the Scripture (2 Timothy 2: 11-13; Hebrews 13:5; Ephesians 1: 13). Permanent indwelling of the Holy Spirit is a special blessing that we receive at the moment of salvation (Colossians 2: 11-12). Even though we have this indwelling of the Holy Spirit, Christians can choose whether or not to be filled with the Holy Spirit. Let me explain this concept.

I believe that there are three reasons why Christians are not filled with the Holy Spirit (Acts 2:4). First of all, Christians are not filled because they do not desire to be filled: they have settled into mediocre 'religion'. Secondly, Christians are not filled because they have quenched the Spirit (1 Thess. 5: 19) by not yielding to the Spirit; by not doing the right things or things of the Spirit. And thirdly, they have grieved the Spirit (Ephesians 4:30). The Holy Spirit of God will not fill an unclean vessel. Doing things that the Holy Spirit would not have us do makes our hearts an unclean vessel. You see, to be filled is to be Spirit-controlled. Do you think that Adam, Alyce, and "Satan's Seven" were Spirit-controlled in their actions at Tiny Town Church?

Christians who are not Spirit-controlled can lose their filling. They lose their filling when disobedience is found (Luke 11:9). The Lord desires that every believer be filled with His Spirit (John 19: 26). How do you do this? You do this by asking to be filled because we can be as filled as we want! And then, after asking, you must yield to the Holy Spirit (Romans 6:13). There is a price to pay, though, when we yield from the world to God;

there is a big price to pay. The Holy Spirit lays claim on us through the Word of God and convicts us of our sins. We then must confess every known sin and we must forsake every known sin. Our filling is lost whenever disobedience is found, and when we fail to ask for forgiveness of our sins. This grieves the Holy Spirit of God. God is grieved by every single un-kind word, deed and thought, un-pure and un-charitable act, all un-true gossip, bitter and un-Christ-like utterance (Ephesians 4: 30). There is one thing I absolutely do not want to do and that is to grieve the Holy Spirit of God!

When we are filled with the Holy Spirit, this leads to being controlled by the Spirit and being controlled by the Spirit leads to true submission, harmony in every relationship, and a meek and mild spirit. I strive for this in my life and in the ministry to which God has called me to serve.

We must always remember that no yielded-ness means no holiness! We don't practice fruit, we bear it. We don't practice joy, we experience it; and we don't practice meekness, we demonstrate it! The Holy Spirit bears fruit in those who walk in the Spirit! Think about what you have read so far about the troubles at Tiny Town Church. Was Alyce walking in the Spirit? Was Adam walking in the Spirit? Were "Satan's Seven" walking in the Spirit? You cannot walk in the Spirit and grieve the Holy Spirit of God, which they all were doing. The problem at Tiny Town Church is felt in our churches across this land, and I am sure it does grieve the Holy Spirit of God[24]!

---

[24] Information learned from lectures and discussions; Master of Arts, Christian Leadership and Master of Divinity degrees, and Doctor of Ministry, Pastoral Leadership degree; *The Doctrine of the Holy Spirit*

9

Trouble in the Church

"...A man reaps what he sows. The one who sows to please his sinful nature, from that nature will reap destruction; the one who sows to please the Spirit, from the Spirit will reap eternal life" (Galatians 6:7-8, NIV).

During my 67 years as a Methodist, I have seen strife, discontent and divisions in our congregations only four times. I have lived in eight states and have been an active part of twelve Methodist congregations, two of which I served as senior pastor. When you look at it statistically, one third of the congregations that I have been a part of have had serious problems. Nationally, 72% of clergy say they know someone who violated someone's boundaries. Crossing boundaries is another prominent problem of a dysfunctional congregation and one that will kill a church.

Crossing boundaries does not have to be sexual. Crossing boundaries is unwanted hugging, being harassed, and performing any kind of close contact or offensive conversations that make the other person feel uncomfortable or violated. In addition, eight out of ten clergywomen have experienced sexual harassment on the job, and one in three congregations have a sexual boundary crossing in its history!!

These statistics are horrible and these problems should not be tolerated. In my personal church history, three of these congregations have witnessed their clergy leadership succumb to sexual misconduct of varying degrees. Four congregations have experienced severe divisions at the hand of the personal agendas of lay and/or clergy leadership. And through all of this I have to wonder: who are we? Are we not following God's agenda anymore? These divisions, personal agendas, gossip, violating one's sacred trust, invading one's space, and pride all lead to devastation among the congregation.

In the early sixties, I remember sitting in church with my family one Sunday morning. I was probably in the eighth or ninth grade. Just before our service started, a black couple was seated in front of us a few rows. I didn't think anything of it because my "other mother" was a black woman whom I loved very much and who had raised me since I was about two years old.

I soon found out that others in that service did not feel that way. Shortly after this couple was seated, several of our prominent families got up and walked out of church, never to return. It was difficult to watch as parents took their children, my friends since birth, out of church. I would never be with these friends again in church activities. This church was divided at the hands of the lay leadership who had their own agenda's and not God's. This time was during the integration period in the south and our bishop had stated that all Methodist Churches were open to everyone of all races and anyone who attended would be seated. As a youngster, I didn't understand about all of this. All I knew was that my friends were taken to another church.

As a young adult in the seventies, this same church was divided again but this time the culprit was the pastor. Our church's parsonage was beautiful, located in an upscale neighborhood and was relatively new. However, the new pastor wanted a parsonage with a swimming pool. I remember this situation to be devastating to the aging congregation because of the liability and expense and prolonged debt. But, after a major screaming and shouting battle in a church meeting, the pastor won. The cost of this win was most of the young, vibrant couples and families of the church. So now, a divided church from the sixties, trying to recover, further divided and lost the young families and most of the children. This church struggled throughout the years but, fortunately, finally now has a pastor who is a good strong leader and is leading this church out of despair and moving forward.

Just after I had entered seminary, we moved to the small town of my mother's birth. The small Methodist church there was eager to welcome us and put us to work. The pastor was a retired elderly pastor hired back as a part-time pastor of two small churches.

We fit in there because everyone knew our family. The pastor was excited that I was studying for the ministry and seemed eager to help me with the candidacy program. He gave me church duties and asked me to lead various study groups. He recruited my husband and me to sing every Sunday. We started a choir and sang in church each week and at all of the special events.

The closer we all became over the next year, the more we began to see odd behaviors in our pastor. He began to use bad and profane language in the sanctuary when he couldn't get his way or when someone objected to his views. We also noticed how he would chastise the congregation, from the pulpit, because the numbers were declining, saying things like "it's your fault people aren't here", and "you'll be sorry if I leave; no one else will pastor this church"!

In addition to this, we noticed very odd behaviors occurring and so our leadership team agreed that it was time to discuss these strange behaviors with him. We gathered together one evening at church and began to voice our concerns. For some reason, he turned on me and began saying things about me that were not true. He screamed at us, gathered up his brief case, and left the meeting and church.

We contacted our supervising clergy, Billy, by letters and emails. He did come and meet with all of us about this one evening. But, Billy passed all of this off as if nothing had happened saying "we go back a long way. Larry is a good friend and pastor." In other words, Billy was telling us that he was covering for his friend's behavior. He failed to listen to the congregation and Larry went on in ministry as if nothing had happened. He turned this incident into anger and lashed out at the members on the leadership team, spreading untrue statements to other members of the congregation, which just about killed the church dead in its tracks! He knew he could hurt me the most because I was in the ministry process so he set out to destroy any chance of my becoming a minister by spreading untrue statements about me to Billy and the ministry committee. I would live with this and battle the scars from this incident throughout my ministry there.

I apologized several times to Larry because I felt badly that he was so angry. He needed professional help but no one would listen. What I didn't know then was that each Supervising Clergy secretly evaluates each student, candidate, and licensed pastor each year before we meet with the district ministry committee for license renewal. The person being evaluated has no idea what was said about them or the results of the evaluation until they are face to face with the committee.

Not long after this incident, I appeared at my yearly ministry committee meeting to evaluate my journey into ministry. The first question asked of me was about the situation with Larry. It was obvious to me that Billy wrote about this incident in my evaluation and based his comments on the accusations of his friend, Larry, and not on the facts and testimony of the other members of the leadership team and congregation. I had a feeling that this would follow me throughout my ministry. And it did. In spite of my tearful explanation, somehow I knew that every clergy around that table were friends with Larry and were supportive of him.

I tried to forget this and move past it and soon buried myself in school and ministry at my first appointment among the true "Saints of God"! We soon got a new supervising clergy, "Jethro", the next year and this subject was never mentioned again. All of my reviews and evaluations were nearly perfect after this incident, and for this I was grateful and blessed.

Later, Larry's situation went from bad to worse and he was arrested and that is another story that maybe he will tell in the future. The Larry situation could have been prevented if Billy had acted on the complaints that were voiced about Larry six years before. How many people could have been spared the hurt and anxiety of division and discontent in the church? And, where is Larry's little church now? It finally has peace, a wonderful pastor, and a church family that is loving and caring. Attendance is struggling to make the mid-double digits but it is regular and everyone finally has peace. I moved on to my first appointment in a small church not far away. I spent many years as pastor there and had a wonderful ministry.

These four cases mentioned here, reflect times when leadership in the church have had their own personal agendas, destroyed lives, relationships and congregations. God's people suffered needlessly. Each church has rules or guidelines to follow, a statement of faith, and maybe even a code of ethics—there is something in place to assist the church in ministry. In the Methodist church it is the **Book of Discipline of the United Methodist Church**.

The **Book of Discipline** is the Methodist rule book for the churches and the employment contract for its clergy. It clearly outlines and describes how we do church as Methodists. The rules mentioned therein are applicable to lay members, lay leadership, clergy, and clergy leadership. We are all bound by the rules of this book.

However, on at least two occasions, I have witnessed a heartbreaking reality. The rules in this book can be forgotten or overlooked, when adverse situations occur. It happened with Larry and it happened again at Tiny Town. This is not unique to the Methodist Church either. For instance, the Catholic Church shared many hours in the news concerning inappropriate behaviors of its priests.

This is politics at work in our churches. It is real and this is the agenda by which many churches move. Did you ever wonder what role the Holy Spirit had in all of this and in the lives of those at Tiny Town? We began discussing the actions of the Holy Spirit in the last chapter and I think we need to continue it here because most people take the action of the Holy Spirit for granted. They totally discount His power and involvement in our daily lives.

The Holy Spirit is the breath of God and is the least understood person of the Godhead. When a person is saved, the moment that person becomes a believer, it is the Holy Spirit that baptizes and saves that person, and permanently indwells that person so that they are now a part of the Body of Christ. A person is saved by the Spirit's work of conviction, conversion, regeneration, baptizing, sealing, and filling. These are the six ministries of the Holy Spirit. When a person is baptized with the Holy Spirit that person is then filled with the Holy Spirit. While the Holy Spirit seals that salvation permanently so that it can never be lost (Ephesians 4:30), the filling can be lost. As baptized Christians, we have to continually be filled with the Spirit (Ephesians 5:18). Our filling can be lost whenever disobedience is found. And, that disobedience grieves the Holy Spirit. In addition, Christians are not filled with the Holy Spirit because they do not desire to be filled or because they have quenched the Spirit (1 Thes. 5:19); The Spirit is quenched when believers do not yield to the Spirit by not doing the right thing or things that are of the Spirit[25].

---

[25] Information learned from lectures and discussions: Master of Arts, Christian Leadership and Master of Divinity degrees, and Doctor of Ministry, Pastoral Leadership degree; *The Doctrine of the Holy Spirit*

Trouble in the church is the result of either lost souls or loss of filling. It would have been impossible to have these problems if all of the people involved had been saved, Baptized in the Holy Spirit, and filled with His Spirit. You cannot yield from the ways of the world and the world's agenda to the Holy Spirit and behave as the characters in this story have done. The action of the Holy Spirit in their lives would not allow that to happen. Each person would have acted differently, Christ-like, considerate, holy and just. The outcome would have been drastically different.

There are many church members and pillars of the church who say they're saved but simply are lost souls. How sad it would be to leave this world in an unsaved state. Are there enough evidences of the Fruit of the Spirit in your life to convince others that you are saved? If we are walking with God, we will manifest God's "fruit garden" everywhere! That is the testimony of holiness in our lives for everyone to see. If we do not manifest God's fruit garden, no one will know for sure if we are saved. The truth is we won't know for sure either.

I have said from the beginning that the solution to the problems of the church today lies in solving the problems of individual Christians. As we have discussed previously, the remedy is a person—the Holy Spirit! *"He is the antidote for every error, the power for every weakness, the victory for every defeat, the supply for every need, and the answer for every question. And He is available to every believer, for He lives in each believer's heart and life"*[26]. The Holy Spirit lives within each of us and He has placed within us all of the answers and the power we need to overcome these difficulties!

---

[26] Ryrie, Charles C. **The Holy Spirit.** 1994. Page 11. Moody Publishers: Chicago.

Divisiveness caused by False Preachers and Teachers

As was mentioned earlier, the problems at Tiny Town Church were certainly Spiritual problems within each of those there. These folks, because of their divisiveness within that local church, as well as within clergy leadership, are considered to be false teachers and preachers. False teachers are members, both teachers and preachers, in the church. We are warned in the scripture to "Beware of false prophets...they are wolves in sheep's clothing..." (Matthew 7: 15). God warns the true believer to watch lest he himself accept false teaching. He must be aware that many deceivers have entered into the world. Believers are to be rewarded for the work they do for Christ but they are in danger of losing that reward if they listen to false teachers and are led astray (2 John 7: 7-8). This reminds me of a story I heard that goes like this:

A city slicker decided to become a farmer. The city slicker bought a farm and moved his family out into the country. The man who sold the farm to the city slicker said: "Mister, it's pretty simple out here. All you have to do is to till the soil, plant the seed, pull the weeds, pray for rain, and then harvest the crop."

The city slicker had gotten a really good deal on the farm and it was plain to see that it was a really good farm with plenty of rich soil and excellent irrigation. By harvest time, the city slicker felt that he would be known as a great farmer! But, this is not the end of the story. You see, during the growing season, the city slicker figured he would save some labor costs and not pull the weeds. He reasoned that the crops would grow faster than the weeds and smother out whatever weeds would shoot up.

But, what he discovered was a rude awakening. When harvest time came, it was one of the saddest days of his life. What should have been a bumper crop of a lifetime turned out to be a lifetime supply of weeds. The city slicker had been given the opportunity of a lifetime but lost it all because the weeds had choked out the crops. He lost it all. He lost his reward. And, in the same sense, the Christian believer can have a field of blessings in store but if false teachers and preachers are allowed to take over, the results will ruin the fruit in the believer's life.

As we discuss these thoughts on false teachers and preachers, one of the biggest roles of these leaders of divisiveness are to reject true ministry and leadership. Immediately I am reminded of the story of Gaius and Diotrephes in 3 John. This story of these two men is very similar to what we experienced at Tiny Town Church, in the clergy leadership mentioned in this and earlier chapters. Gaius was well loved (vs 1). John deeply loved Gaius. Their close bond was Jesus Christ. He truly lived for Christ. Gaius prospered spiritually in spite of ill health (vs 2). He suffered illness and John wanted him to know that he was praying for him. Gaius was growing in the fruit of the Spirit and he prospered. Spiritual prosperity comes from faithfully doing the will of God.

Gaius walked in the truth (vs. 3-4). John praised Gaius for one particular aspect of his walking in the truth, namely, that he had been faithful in helping traveling missionaries. Gaius had a strong testimony. He patterned his life after Jesus Christ himself and he brought joy to the hearts of the believers. John was joyous of the life Gaius was living. Gaius stood up for the truth. He stood up against those who were destroying their church through their divisiveness. He approached them in God's love, the way Jesus Christ would approach them.

Gaius helped Christian believers and missionaries and strangers (vs. 5-8). He supplied them with lodging, food, money, and whatever other help they needed for their journey. His commitment to the missionary cause of Christ was so impressive that missionaries had specifically mentioned it to John (vs. 6). Gaius's action toward these preachers of the gospel came from his love for them, for the gospel, and for those without Christ. Gaius had a strong ministry in hospitality. According to what is written here, all church congregations are to support those who are chosen by God to preach His word.

It is a duty and a privilege of God's people to contribute to missionary needs and work. Receiving, sending, and supporting missionaries must be done in a manner worthy of God. They must not be treated like beggars, but must be received as the Lord (Matt. 10:40) and as his servants carrying the gospel to all the world. The sending of missionaries in the early church consisted of providing for their journey and supplying them with food and money to pay expenses and live adequately. By supporting missionaries, God's people became fellow helpers in spreading the truth (vs. 8). Spiritual leaders are chosen to lead people to Christ and they are to be held up and encouraged.

The people of God must defeat the schemes of the divisive church leader: Just as God sends key people to strengthen the church, Satan also sends his agents to suck the life out of the church. A divisive church leader has left his fingerprint of chaos on more than one church. A divisive leader is one of the most serious problems that ever confront the church. When a church has within its ranks a divisive leader, the very life and ministry of the church are threatened.

A divisive leader always carries the church through the most traumatic experiences. This person usually gathers others around him in a clique of opposition, and when he goes this far he becomes much more of a threat to the life of the church. This was the exact pattern that "Satan's Seven plus two" followed at Tiny Town Church.

Now, Diotrephes' legacy was that of division. He was known as a divisive church leader who wanted to be first in the church; he wanted to be the most important person; he wanted everyone to come to him first before consulting the pastor of the church. He desired to rule the whole church. He rejected leadership from colleagues, and he rejected John's authority. He rejected the appointed authority of the church, and he was bitter and divisive. He showed others he opposed the minister of the church, and he opposed those who stood behind the minister. He was so strong in his opposition that he drove people away from the church. He was disturbing every facet of church life. He was affecting the church's outreach. These things and more are what happen when a divisive leader is within the church. A divisive leader is not to be followed. He may be a leader; he may even be high up in the leadership ladder, but His leadership is to be rejected if he is sowing seeds of divisiveness and undermining the ministry of the church. No matter who he is; no matter what his position is in the church. The divisive leader is not born of God, for God is always Good.

Diotrephes was prideful. He did not receive them well and he "loveth to have the preeminence among them" (vs. 9). He "was prating against us with malicious words: and not content therewith"; he did not receive the brethren and forbid the others who wanted to. He cast them out of the church. He was selfish, self-centered, and did not have the love of God within his heart.

The Godly leader, maybe the minister who was being sent to the church to straighten it out, was known to be a godly person and for walking in the truth. This godly servant of the Lord strived to walk with the Lord and to uphold the rules of the church. He was willing to deal with the problems of the church because his life was rooted in Christ. A divisive leader is like a cancer to the church. A divisive church leader can certainly destroy the church. Don't focus on your Diotrephes in your church: focus on your Gaius (3 John 1-9)!

You might ask the question: What can the believer do if we know that our leaders are divisive or false teachers or preachers? 1 John 4: 1-6 lists several things the believer must do. These are:

1. Testing the spirits of teachers (vs. 1). The false teacher is like quicksand, waiting to suck you in. If you are following the spirit of a true teacher or preacher, then it is a true indication that you love God. If you are following the spirit of a false teacher or preacher, then it is a true indication that you do not love God.

Believers can be misled by the spirits of false teachers or preachers. What kind of spirits are these?

   a. He may have a spirit of lie. He may present a way of life that is good and a blessing

b. He may have a spirit of righteousness. He may preach and teach righteousness that stresses morality, giving, serving, etc.
c. He may stress the qualities of the life of Jesus Christ. But, in reality, what this person teaches or preaches is a lie. They live a different life than what they teach or preach about. There are many false preachers and teachers in our churches around the world. They are talking the talk but not walking the walk. They are often the ones who are the most vocal, calling attention to themselves. Many times, they are the leaders of the denominations, the churches, and the very people of God. They are deceitful workers of God and their end shall be according to their work. Their very motivation is to hold back the church of God!

2. Test the confession of teachers (vs. 2-3). What is it that makes a preacher or teacher true or false? Jesus Christ is the answer. What a man believes about Jesus Christ makes a teacher or preacher true or false. What a man confesses exposes his heart. The Spirit of God confesses the truth!
3. Test yourselves (vs. 4). Ask yourself if you are of God. Have you had a rebirth in Christ? Are you overcoming the false spirits of this world?
4. Test the followers of teachers (5-6). Look at the people who follow these teachers or preachers. These people are worldly. False teachers and preachers are of the world so they attract worldly followers. They teach a worldly view of God: that man reaches God by being good and doing

good; that man reaches God by going to church, doing the rituals of the church, and by doing good. These approaches focus on man and what he does; not on God or what God does. They are centered in the world and not on God. They fail to take a stand for God and His church; they fail to live boldly for Christ!

Adam and Alyce, in their quest to protect the misdeeds of Larry, Alyce, Pastor Kim, Jodie, and the rest of "Satan's Seven, not only failed to live boldly for Christ, but they also became divisive leaders and workers because of their fear—fear of being discovered and overcome.

Fear does terrible things to us, doesn't it? It actually causes us to make fools of ourselves. It limits our aspirations and it makes us see and feel things that are not there and/or are untrue. I wonder how many of us give in to the bondage of fear! The folks involved in this anarchy at Tiny Town sure did. Fear has crippled so many lives. Fear keeps us in bondage! Romans 8: 15 (NIV) says, "For you have not received the spirit of bondage again to fear; but you have received the Spirit of adoption…" That means that fear is our enemy and it distorts reality. I often think how many times in the scriptures I have read the words, "Fear not!" Christ is telling us to have faith…to believe and not to fear. The call to follow Christ is definitely a call to boldness. It is a call to let our light shine, to be full of courage, faith and truth. You see, the opposite of faith is fear! Fear is our enemy. Look what the fear of knowing the truth about Larry and Alyce did. It caused both of them to have a distorted understanding of the reality of the situation. It caused them to believe things about me that just were not the truth. Fear destroys lives. And, at Tiny Town Church, it did just that!

One of my favorite books is **Story Journey**[27]. In this book, the author tells a story about a very frightening experience that happened when he was about ten years old. Tom and his friend, Jim, were out sledding in a park not far from his home. The park was about a half mile wide and it was located in the middle of town. It was surrounded by a wooded area on one side and a cemetery and an open field on the other side. On this particular day, it was a cold wintery day where you could see those long shadows on the snow that were cast from the clouds above. Most of the time, there were a lot of kids out sledding, but on this particular afternoon, Tom and Jim were the only kids out in the park.

At one point in their sledding, Jim yelled to Tom, "Hey Boomer, did you see that over there in the cemetery? It looked like something was moving!" That got Tom's attention and he looked out over the valley but saw nothing but the trees and tombstones. Soon, his friend continued, "It must have just been my imagination; but I'd swear that I saw something moving over there!"

Well, needless to say, that after that brief conversation, the fun had totally vanished and both boys were now afraid. They kept on sledding and tried to have fun and be cheerful, but it was no use. They could not be cheerful—they were both scared! Now, as if enough had not been said, Jim shouted again, "Look! It's a panther!" Well, scared to death, Tom looked. And, he swears to this day that he saw a huge black panther running through the

---

[27] Thomas E. Boomershine. **Story Journey,** Nashville: Abingdon Press, 1988. Pages 99-101

cemetery, leaping over the fence and across the snow-covered field right toward them. Both boys turned and ran as fast as they could, afraid for their very lives!

As Tom ran through the woods he could hear the panther getting closer and closer behind him. He was so afraid. As he got close to his house he tripped over his sled and fell into the snow. He just knew he had had it! He knew it was over. He waited to feel that panther on his back with his hot breath on his neck and his claws digging into his back. But, to his surprise, nothing happened. He got up and ran into his house. He told his mother what had happened. His mother assured him that there was no panther; there had never been a panther at all[28].

What had happened was this: both of these boys' imaginations had been working overtime. There was no real danger at all. However, they sure thought there was, and they experienced real life-threatening fear! You see, when we fear, we have a false view of reality. Fear makes us actually give up before we even get started. It causes us to get off course and take an alternate route rather than the direct path toward our destination. We tend to see obstacles rather than the opportunities before us. All of reality is distorted. The reality and truth surrounding my understanding and knowledge of Larry's and Alyce's secrets were severely distorted and both of them actually believed something that was not true. Fear is our enemy. It distorts reality!

So, how do we free ourselves from this bondage to fear? Well, we first have to understand that fear is a spiritual problem! It is the opposite of Faith. It is our enemy! We need to know this and

---

[28] IBID; Thomas E. Boomershine

we then need to make a commitment to living boldly for Christ. We need to understand that fear is contrary to the call of Christ! These divisive leaders acted out of unfounded fear because they knew that they were hiding sin.

Divisive leadership can and will suck the life out of the church and will destroy its ministry. It is truly the work of Satan at the highest level and it must be overcome. So, how does a believer overcome Satan? I have listed ten ways, with scriptural references:

1. By drawing near to God and praying and asking for wisdom (James 1:5)
2. By using God's Word—quoting it over and over again in their minds to conquer temptations (Luke 4:8)
3. By learning and knowing that God allows temptation to teach endurance (James 1: 2-3)
4. By not yielding their bodily members to sin (Romans 6: 13)
5. By clothing themselves with the armor of God (Ephesians 6: 13)
6. By keeping on guard—being on guard—and waiting for the tempter's temptations (1 Peter 5:8)
7. By not giving in to anger or giving place to the devil (Ephes. 4: 26-27)
8. By submitting to God and resisting the devil (James 4:7)
9. By not giving in to the enticement of sinners (Proverbs 1:10)
10. By not entering in the path of the wicked (Proverbs 4: 14)

All of this is done in light of Revelations 12: 11: *"and they overcome him, Satan, by the blood of the Lamb and by the Word of their testimony, and they love not their lives unto the death"*. So, the way we overcome Satan, in light of the above ten ways mentioned is characterized by saying that we overcome by the blood of the Lamb and our testimony of what Jesus Christ has done for us. Satan stays after the believer as long as he/she is on this earth. A mature believer overcomes and continues to fight Satan with the Word of God[29]. We must overcome Satan and eliminate his warriors who have vowed to destroy the church and its vision and mission. And, it does not start at the bottom of the ladder (the local church). Change starts at the top. Our churches need a revival and it has to start with the clergy leadership. If the clergy fail to lead by God's agenda, how can we ever expect to rid our congregations of the devils who infiltrate them?

---

[29] Information learned from lectures and discussions: Master of Arts, Christian Leadership and Master of Divinity degrees; and Doctor of Ministry, Pastoral Leadership degree; *The Doctrine of the Holy Spirit*

Healing and Moving Forward

"So I have come down to rescue them from the hand of the Egyptians and to bring them up out of that land into a good and spacious land, a land flowing with milk and honey..." (Exodus 3:8, NIV)

Higher Ground

I'm pressing on the upward way, New Heights I'm gaining every day;
Still praying as I onward bound, "Lord, plant my feet on higher ground."

My heart has no desire to stay where doubts arise and fears dismay;
Tho' some may dwell where these abound, my
prayer, my aim, is higher ground.

I want to live above the world, tho' Satan's darts at me are hurled;
For faith has caught the joyful sound, the
song of saints on higher ground!

Lord, Lift me up and let me stand, by faith, on Heaven's table-land,
A higher plane than I have found; Lord,
plant my feet on higher ground[30].

---

[30] www.hymnary.org. Words by Johnson Oatman, Jr., 1898. Copyright: Public Domain. Based on the Scripture from Deuteronomy 32:13. Music by Charles H. Gabriel, 1902. Copyright: Public Domain.

10

We'll Just Call You Sister
The Love of God and Loving One Another

"Dear friends, let us love one another, for love comes from God. Everyone who loves has been born of God and knows God. Whoever does not love does not know God, because God is love" (1 John 4: 7-8, NIV).

Several months prior to the abrupt termination of my ministry at Tiny Town Church, our church and other churches in the area began lifting our voices to God in one of the most amazing acts of praise in which I had ever participated. Anyone who could play a musical instrument would bring it and merge their talent with the others on the stage. The music that was produced was truly amazing. Those who wanted to, sang their special songs and others led the congregation in all of the old-time favorites. There was never a doubt that the Holy Spirit was alive and moving throughout every single person there. Our church hosted a couple of these "Sings", but most were held at *"The Bible Church"*.

During those several months that we attended and participated in the Gospel Sings, I became acquainted with the pastor, and his family, as well as the many wonderful and loving folks who worshiped there. The week after my ministry was terminated at Tiny Town Church, I was invited by my close friends to attend the monthly Gospel Sing at *The Bible Church*. I really did not feel like seeing anyone and I surely did not feel like singing. I was grieving. I was trying to sort all of this out. I felt alone, abandoned by my once supportive congregation and denomination, and empty; totally empty. But, I went anyway. And, I am so glad I did.

While I did not feel like singing in front of the group, I still needed to be in their midst. When I walked through the front door, I felt as though I was home. The pastor and his wife met our group as we walked in. My dear friend went first and introduced me to them as "her pastor, Rev. Sophie Baker". The pastor, knowing all about what had happened at Tiny Town Church, hugged me and said, "We'll just call you Sister; you are one of us now!" My heart was full and my soul came alive with thanksgiving. God had placed me there at that particular time. I needed them. I needed a pastor whom I could talk to. I needed someone who was Spirit-filled and who could help me sort out this situation. God placed me there and I knew I was home. From then on, they all lovingly called me "Sister Sophie"!

Even after we moved out of the parsonage at Tiny Town Church and on to our new ministry setting, my husband and I continued to attend the Gospel Sings at *The Bible Church*. They have become a very important part of our lives and we consider the congregation there to be our church family and the church to be our church. Since I had no pastor, my new friend filled that position. He became my mentor, my spiritual guide, my colleague, and my dear friend. I could not have recovered from the grief and trauma I suffered at Tiny Town without his guidance and love. The love that I felt when I was in the midst of the good people of *The Bible Church* was truly a special and an amazing thing. I have never felt this before in a congregation of people. It was God's love: It is God's love!

Have you experienced God's love? What I learned was that God loves you, but you have to enter into a loving relationship with God in order to experience His love for you! If you do not love God you will never know or experience His love for you. This was missing at Tiny Town Church: there was no love flowing between most of the worshipers and God. God's love was there but theirs was not. You just could not feel it.

I have spent nearly two years sorting all of this out, and I have come to realize that the folks who truly had a relationship with God at Tiny Town Church could be counted on the fingers of my hands. And most of those Godly few are no longer there. I also came to realize that very few people really know and walk with God. This includes clergy, clergy leadership, as well as members of our congregations. I found that most are confused with terminology. They call themselves "Christians" because they go to church and they may even hold high positions in the church, but they do not walk with God: they are not in fellowship with God.

Before we go further, let's discuss three terms of confusion. First, "Christian", in the broad sense, means that a person believes in Christ. It does not mean that they follow Scriptural teachings, the Ten Commandments, study their Bible or even go to church. That person is known to be a "believer". Now, there are two types of "believers". There is the believer who is in fellowship with God and there is the one who is not. There are many who are not. While reading the following pages, it will become clear, according to the Scripture, what the requirements are for being in the fellowship of God through our Lord Jesus Christ.

Few people truly know God. It is so sad, but they have to walk through life without knowing God's love and without knowing God's care. They have to face all of the trials and temptations of life all alone. They have no help except what man can give. They have rejected the help and love of God. They have to face suffering and sorrow and the death of loved ones all alone. They do not have the supernatural power of God to help because they have rejected His love. They have to confront death without really knowing if God is on the other side waiting to judge them. They have no hope beyond this life, feeling that this life may be all, but not quite sure; and they wonder if there is something after death, but not being sure. Thanks be to God—God loves the world and all who dwell therein—therefore, any of us who want to know God's love and care can do so. All we have to do is respond to His love; open our hearts and lives and receive His love and love Him in return!

In a society that is marked by indifference, one of the most difficult obstacles for a believer is to live out a life marked by genuine love and concern for others. Loving God and loving others must be a daily effort in a culture that puts the 'self' first; and in a culture that can be indifferent to the pain and sorrow of others. Indifference is worse than hate because indifference requires no effort at all; it is cold; it is uncaring; it is unloving. In the following paragraphs, I have listed some Biblical thoughts about "love". Please study these carefully and prayerfully, remembering the actions of the characters of this story of Tiny Town Church.

- <u>You cannot love God if you do not love others</u>. If you hold feelings against anyone, this is clear proof that you do not love God! The great mark of loving God is the mark of loving others.
- Love shows if you are a child of God or of the devil (1 John 3: 10): the person who does not love his brother or mistreats, abuses, neglects, ignores his brother is not of God. The person who does not live a holy life is not of God.
- Love is the message heard from the very beginning (vs 11): love one another;
- Righteousness is love. Unrighteousness is the failure to love.
- Love is righteous deeds in action.
- Love is the message we have heard from the beginning because we need each other; we are a lonely society.
- Loving one another is not an option; it is a command.
- Love does not persecute the righteous (vs 12-13) people. A person who loves will not criticize, back bite, gossip, censor, spread rumors, downgrade, attack, abuse, be envious, dislike, talk about, stand against, hurt, destroy, murder, oppose or hate.
- Love means that we will not even dislike others. We love them and we want them to reach the fullness in Christ. We must not persecute our brother.
- Love is the fruit that proves that one has passed from death to life (vs 14): This refers to both spiritual death while still living in this natural world and physical death. A person who wastes his life in non-spiritual living is spiritually dead. A person who has not become one with Christ is

spiritually dead. A person who does not have the love of Christ in him is spiritually dead; a person who lives in sin is said to be spiritually dead; a person who is alienated from God is spiritually dead; a person who sleeps in sin is spiritually dead; a person who lives in sinful pleasure is spiritually dead; a person who does not have the Son of God is spiritually dead; and a person who does great religious work but does the wrong works is spiritually dead (Rev. 3:1).

- We must love our pastors.
- We must love each other.
- Love does not hate (1 John 3: 15): you cannot love your brother and back-bite, gossip, participate in gossip and evil deeds against your brother and still be in fellowship with God. Many people feel that they can treat others any way they want to, and still be in favor with God. They have feelings of hate, bitterness, anger, dislike, unwillingness to get along, get-even attitude; they gossip about and do evil deeds against their neighbor and still think they walk with God. This is just not so. These things equal hate in God's eyes and you cannot hate your brother. Love is the only security against hate. Anyone who does not love hates. The person who does not love his brother does not walk in fellowship with God. The participants at Tiny Town were involved in these hateful behaviors aimed at the destruction of God's ministry and people. Love was never shown by them. Bitterness, anger, dislike and evil filled their hearts instead. They did not have a clean heart and therefore, could not be in fellowship with God.

- Love is the fruit that one understands the love of Christ (vs 16). Christ died for us when we were ungodly, without strength, when we were sinners in rebellion to God. In spite of all of our sins, Christ died for us because He loved us. We can prove the love of Christ when we do good to those who mistreat us. This is one of the hardest things to do.
- Love has compassion and gives to meet the needs of people (vs 17). The love of God does not dwell within a person who fails to help a person he sees in need. If we fail to help others and give to others, how can we say we have the love of God within us? The believer never loses when the motivation is love (2 Cor. 8: 12-13).

Having a Clean Heart

If you truly love God you will have a clean heart. I believe that a clean heart is brought about by loving in deed and not in word only (1 John 3: 18-19). Think on these things:

- The love we are to have is the love for our enemies and those we do not like as well as for our friends and those we like.
- We are to love like God loves. We are to love those who do evil as well as those who are holy and we must love all of those who oppose us. This will bring us assurance.
- A clean heart is brought about by God's knowledge (vs. 20, 21). God has made our hearts sensitive so we will know wrongdoing. He did this so we will know when we sin.

God knows all of our decisions even when we don't make them, and He knows what we would have done in other circumstances. Nothing can be hidden from God.

- A clean heart is brought about by keeping God's commandments (vs. 22). We must obey our Father if we are going to please Him because God will not reward our unfaithfulness. If we expect our sins to be forgiven, we must obey God in order to please Him, and if we do sin, we must ask for forgiveness. The only way we can be in fellowship with God is to ask for forgiveness of our sins. And then, God will reward us if we do two things: Keep his commandments and love our neighbor.
- A clean heart is brought about by keeping the supreme commandment of God (vs. 23). That is, to believe in the Lord Jesus Christ and love your neighbor. This means to believe in all that Jesus Christ stands for and who he is and what he is. This is the foundation of life and this is the only way we become pleasing before God. Keeping this commandment is the very first thing a person has to do, and must do, in order to please God and have a clean heart. This all happens through love—love is the key. We must love all others.

A clean heart is brought about by the spirit dwelling within (vs. 24). The person who believes in Jesus Christ and loves others dwells in God and God in him. He abides in us through the Holy Spirit. We must live and walk in God: we must make our home in God; we must take up residence in God. God then lives within us. He makes his home within us. He is our constant companion.

Every Christian has the Holy Spirit within. It is sad that some take Him to places of shame and expose Him to attitudes and conversations that hurt Him greatly. This grieves the Holy Spirit of God. We need to replace this sin within us with more of Him. When there is more of Christ within you than you within you, then your heart will be full of the Holy Spirit.

Loving Others

Do you love others? Do you really love your fellow man? Do you love your neighbor, no matter who he is? Loving others proves that we are born of God and know God (1 John 4: 7-8): because God is love. If a person really loves God, they have the nature of God. They love others as God loves them. And, others will see that they live Godly lives. If a person does not live a godly life and love others as God does, he does not know God.

Let's look at what loving others proves to us:

- Loving others proves that we see God's love (vs. 9-11): God is love and he has proven his love by sending Jesus Christ in this world. We know that God loves us because he saves us from our sins. And, because God loves us we should love others. We are to love everyone even those who do not love us, and even those who are hard to love. There are times we are all hard to love but, still, God loves us and he has sent Jesus Christ to die for our sins. We are to show others the way of the cross.
- Loving others proves that God's Spirit is within us (vs. 12-13): No one has ever seen God. He is only known by

love and by His Spirit that is within believers. God plants his divine nature in the life of the believer and he begins to dwell in us so that His Son, Jesus Christ will have many followers, followers who will honor Him and live and love just as Christ lived and loved. Then God's love becomes pure and perfected in us.

- Loving others proves that our testimony and confession are true (vs. 14-16): This is John's testimony as stated in the scripture; this is the testimony of John himself. God is love therefore if we do not love others we do not have the nature of God within us.
- Loving others proves that God is going to deliver us from judgment (vs. 17): If we love perfectly, we will have boldness in the Day of Judgment and we shall be rewarded. We are to love just as Christ loved. This should be our consuming passion (Hebrews 4:16).
- Loving others proves that God delivers us from fear (1 John 4:18): There is no fear in love. God promises that if we truly love, we will not fear Him; he will give us a deep peace and assurance of sole that erases all fear. There is no fear in love: perfect love cast out all fear. A believer cannot love one person and hold ill-feelings against another person. A heart cannot hold both love and hate. It is incompatible. Fear means that one is not perfected in love. Fear can be cast out only by the perfect love of God. There is no need to fear people for God comforts us. There is no need to fear judgment for God

delivers us from judgment. There is no need to fear the enemies of the dark for God will take care of us. God is our shield. There is no need to fear anything: Matthew 6: 25-31.

- Loving others proves that we love God (1 John 4: 19-21): We love him because He first loved us. We know that God loves us because we love our brothers. We know that God loves us because we love Him and keep His commandments. Jesus Christ came into this world to save people not institutions. This should be our focus in ministry and missions. When religious institutions lose their primary concern for the spiritual and temporary needs of people, heaven weeps and the zest to carry on fades and dies. Such institutions become soul-less and are a distorted image of what they ought to be. Our major emphasis must always be on people. We must have love and respect for people everywhere and have a concern for them, always wanting the highest and best welfare for them.
- Loving one another proves the above seven points, and it proves that you love God. We must believe Jesus is the Christ. We must love God and keep His commandments. We must strive to do what God says; and, we must know when we don't. Our obedience to God shows that we love our brothers and sisters in Christ. Our obedience to God proves our love for God. Jesus Christ gives rest to the soul when one is in fellowship with Him.

Whoever believes that Jesus is the Christ is born of God, and everyone who is born of God must overcome the world (1 John 5:4-5):

1. The person who overcomes the world is the person who is born of God (vs. 4)
2. The victory that overcomes the world our faith (vs. 4)
3. The person who overcomes is the person who believes that Jesus is the Son of God (vs. 5).

I want to continue these thoughts about love. I have mentioned above what scripture says about having a clean heart and loving others, but what IS love? I love the description given in II John 6. In this chapter, John was concerned about false teachers and those who were mistreating his dear friend. She refused to open her house to these false teachers. She was being mistreated and abused. John tells the lady to love them. We are to love them that mistreat us. Love them. Man has always thought that he was to love his friends. This is easy to do. But, this lady was being told to love those who mistreat her; to love as God loves.

John loves and cares for others in a way consistent with NT revelation about Christ. It is possible to show love toward others, yet not be committed to the truth of God's Word. Such persons place love, acceptance, friendship, and unity above the truth and commandments of God (vs. 5-6). On the other hand, it is possible for a person in the church to promote Biblical truth and defend its doctrines, yet not show love and concern for others. What God requires is that we demonstrate both love for His truth and love for others. We must speak the truth in love. 1 Corinthians 13: 6

describes love as an activity and a behavior, not just as an inner feeling or motivation. The various aspects of love included here characterize God the Father, Son and Holy Spirit. Since this is so, every believer must seek to grow in this kind of love. Christ loved us and gave himself for us even when we did not deserve it. We must love one another, no matter who it is. We must love just as the Word of God says to love. If we know Christ, then Christ and the Holy Spirit live within us, and as a result, we will love others. Love is not an option. Believers must love. Love is a behavior; a way of life. Love is obedience.

There are several scriptures that I frequently use in wedding ceremonies that I am sure you have all heard at one time or another. See if this sounds familiar to you. In the Scriptures, the Bible gives us these great examples of what love really is. Love suffers a long, long time no matter what evil has been done by a person. Love controls itself. Love is patient with people not with circumstances. Love suffers without seeking revenge or getting even. Love does not resent; does not envy; it is not jealous. Love does not attack or downgrade the abilities of others. Love is not boastful; it does not seek to get attention or glory. Love is not prideful or conceited. Love is modest and humble. Love does not shame one's self. Love is not selfish. Love is not easily angered or quick tempered; it controls the emotions. Love does not think evil; does not consider the wrong suffered; is not resentful; does not hold the wrong done to self (1 Corinthians 13:4-7; Matthew 5: 39). Love suffers the wrong done to self and then forgets all about it; it does not strive to get even with those you perceived to have wronged you. Love does not feed upon sin and wrong; gossip, back-biting, get-even tactics. Love does not rush to tell some the misfortune of others. Christians have the obligations to speak guardedly in love and kindness.

Love rejoices in the truth. It rejoices when the truth is rooted in each individual. Love bears all things. Love stands up under the weight of all things and it covers up the faults of others. It has no pleasure in exposing the faults and wrongs of others (Ephesians 4: 2-3). Love believes all things, is totally trusting, is willing to believe the best, accepts and believes the best in others. Love hopes all things, expects the good to eventually triumph; it refuses to accept failure, and hopes for the best. Love endures all things; love is strong and conquers all things. Love is an action word. Love is a way of life. We are commanded to love[31].

If a person is living a pure and holy life, if they love every person in their life, and if they truly have a clean heart, it is not possible to participate in unloving behaviors or to treat a minister of God, called of God into service, the way the clergy leadership and their group of followers did at Tiny Town. It is just not possible!

---

[31] Information learned from lectures and discussions: Master of Arts, Christian Leadership and Master of Divinity degrees; Doctor of Ministry, Pastoral Leadership degree; *1 John-Jude*

11

Living in the Spirit

"Do not love the world or anything in the world. If anyone loves the world, the love of the Father is not in him. For everything in the world—the cravings of sinful man, the lust of his eyes and the boasting of what he has and does—comes not from the Father but from the world. The world and its desires pass away, but the man who does the will of God lives forever" (1 John 2: 15-17, NIV).

The world does not know or understand "believers". When I speak of "believers" here, I am referring to the body of Christ who are walking in fellowship with Him. This explains why we believers are ridiculed, mocked, made fun of, ignored, opposed, abused, rejected and persecuted by "the world", or those outside of the fellowship of Christ. This is sad to say, but this persecution may come at work; it may come at school, or in the neighborhood; or it may even come in our churches. The world just doesn't understand why we act and live the way we do. I encountered all of these behaviors in the Tiny Town Church among the group I have referred to as "Satan's Seven", as well as in the clergy and lay leadership.

This group of 'seven plus two' is not unique to the Tiny Town Church community. These groups of devils are wreaking havoc in many of our congregations across the land. They represent 'the world' and how it believes and lives. The world does not understand why we separate ourselves from the pleasures and things of the world. The world does not understand why we deny ourselves and live sacrificially so we can carry the message of Christ to the world, meeting the needs of the desperate! And, the world does not understand why we worship so much and talk so much about Christ. The world just does not know Jesus Christ and it is unwilling to recognize and acknowledge that God is righteous, pure and just. They want nothing to do with the lifestyle that demands all that a person is and has! They are just not willing to give sacrificially to carry the Gospel around the world and to meet the needs of the world.

Most folks who attend our worship services, who work in our churches, who are considered serving in leadership roles, and those who are in clergy leadership at all levels, just do not understand the nature of believers; that we are the children of God and can lead no other life than following God. It is difficult for them to understand our commitment to God to withdraw from the world and worldly living (Matthew 10:17). I cannot think, however, of any other way to live than to live for God and by His Word!

So, my question is this: do you love the world? The believer that loves the world does not love God. What is meant by the 'world'? Does this mean that we are not to enjoy our blessings and the beauty all around us? Absolutely not! What does it mean, then?

The 'world' means the earth and the heavens that are passing away. The world is corruptible and the world is deteriorating.

Because of this, the world will eventually be destroyed. Believers must not become attached to the world. They must be attached to God and they must be attached to heaven. Believers are not to love the world so much that they desire to stay here more than they desire to be with God in heaven. I remember when I was a young girl; I would become so sad when I thought of dying and when I thought of all of our family who has died. I could not imagine what life would be like here on earth without me here. As I got older, I would think how sad it was that people die and leave this earth. But, once I began living for Christ, I realized that this earthly life is just a practice run for the really wonderful life that is waiting for all of us who live for Christ and His kingdom now.

As I have grown in Christ, I have realized that the world is a system of man-made governments and societies. Some are good and some are bad. But none are perfect. Unfortunately, our church systems are also included in this. Therefore, believers must respect and be loyal to the good but reject and stand against the bad. Believers must love none of them—not to the point that they are more attached to the systems of man's organizations than they are to God and heaven!

Lastly, the 'world' means a system of sin. It means a system of lust and evil pride and rebellion against God. The world is full of sinful people; people who are evil; people who are full of lust; people who are full of pride; people who are in a rebellion against God. Therefore, believers must not live this sinful system of the world. So, when the Bible speaks about love not the world, it's talking about the system of the world. A person is not to love the world: the possessions and pleasures of this world. He is to love God! He is to appreciate the gifts and blessings from God, but is not to become more attached to the things of this world than he is to God and to heaven! We are to love God above all else (Romans 12:2)! We have made a promise to God when we accepted Him into our hearts to resist these evil temptations and prideful acts. If we truly love God, we will!

This reminds me of a story my professor told in class about a missionary. In his mission field, this missionary had to do many things for himself and for his family. When the baby grew too big for the carriage, he had to build a bed for the child. He started to prepare the wood for the bed. He glued the wood pieces together and was ready to complete the bed. His wife thought it too cold to work in the shed, so he brought the pieces of the bed into the kitchen to work. When the bed was finished, the baby was brought to the kitchen and placed in it and his parents looked on admiringly. And suddenly, the father had a disquieting thought: suppose the bed would not go through the door. Quickly he measured the door and found that the bed was 1 inch too wide to pass through.

There are many people who spend their time building their lives to the plan of this world. They take great pride in their work. The day will come when they suddenly realize that the measurements will not allow them to pass through heaven's door. I certainly hope that you are not one of them.

The Holy Spirit

I can only imagine how grieved the Spirit must be over the actions of Adam, Alyce and the gossip group at Tiny Town. There are only three institutions God has ordained on Earth (Ephesians

2: 19-22). These are Marriage, Human Government and the Church. Of these three, the church is the most important to the Holy Spirit. The Holy Spirit was definitely grieved. Most folks don't clearly understand the Holy Spirit and His actions in the church and our lives. I want to spend the next part of this chapter discussing this because I believe that the lack of being filled with the Holy Spirit and being out of fellowship with God created the sins that are the root of the problem at Tiny Town Church and most of our churches today. This lack of filling pertains not only to the Church Body, but also to the clergy and lay leadership.

The Holy Spirit has five actions in the church: inspires the worship service (Philippians 3: 3-4), directs missionary work (Acts 13:2; 16:6-7, 10), directs and aids in its singing services (Ephesians 5:18), appoints its preachers (Acts 20:28), and anoints its preachers (Acts 10: 38, 15: 38; 1 Timothy 1:12, 3; 1 Cor. 2:4). So when the Holy Spirit is not present, when ministry, missions, or singing in the church seems dead or empty, it is because these are being performed of the flesh not allowing the Holy Spirit to direct and bless His ministries. Works of the flesh are present when those who serve or worship are not yielded to the Holy Spirit. Servants should be chosen, not on ability alone, but on yielded-ness to the Holy Spirit. Yielded-ness produces Fruit!

Fruit of the Holy Spirit is different from Spiritual Gifts. Spiritual Gifts are given by Christ to the believer at the time of conversion. Every believer has at least one Gift and that is Christ's abiding presence, His permanent indwelling (John 14:6). Spiritual Gifts were given first at Pentecost on an individual basis to each believer, and are given to each believer at the Holy Spirit's discretion to empower the believer to do the work God has given him to do (1 Cor. 12: 4-11). The purpose of spiritual gifts is to glorify the Father and to edify the church (Psalm 34:3; 1 Cor. 14:12). So, the ultimate goal of the Holy Spirit here on this earth is to bear fruit for Christ through believers (Romans 6:22)! Sadly, we can abuse these spiritual gifts too. They can be abused by not using the gifts that are given to you or by preventing someone else from using their gifts, as they did at Tiny Town (1 Timothy 4:14); by counterfeiting the sign gifts—pretending to perform a miracle, healing or to speak in or interpret tongues (Proverbs 25: 14); or by not using the gifts in love (1 Corinthians 13:1).

However, as believers, we are commanded in the Scripture to *bear fruit* (Gen. 1:28; 49:22; Psalm 1:3; Rev. 22: 1-2). But, in order to bear fruit, one must die to this world (must withdraw from the sinful and wicked ways of this world), must abide in the Savior (strive to live a life pleasing to God), and must yield to the Spirit (John 12: 24) (must eliminate the works of the flesh in the Christian's life). You may be asking "what types of fruit are we to produce"? Well, the NT speaks of several different kinds of fruit. I will list these for you:

- Souls won to Christ (John 4: 35-36; Proverbs 11: 30; Romans 1: 13)
- Holy Living (Romans 6: 22)
- Gifts brought to God (Romans 15: 26-28)
- Good Works (Colossians 1:10; Ephesians 2:10)
- Praise (Hebrews 13:15)
- Christian Character (Ephesians 5:9; Galatians 5: 22-23)

These kinds of fruit will result when we obtain the nine attributes in our lives: love, joy, peace, longsuffering (patience and endurance), gentleness, goodness, faith, meekness and temperance. All nine attributes are to be displaced in the life of the believer. These are not "fruits" of the spirit, but are attributes that make up the Fruit of the Spirit. A believer must contain all nine attributes in order to contain the Fruit of the Spirit. In addition to these nine attributes, there are seventeen works of the flesh. If you contain any of these, then you do not have the Fruit of the Spirit. This is a little scary, isn't it?

The purpose of the Fruit of the Spirit is three-fold: to magnify the Lord Jesus Christ, to give testimony to the transformed life, and to show the work of God in the believer's life (Psalm 29:2). It is not possible for the believer to obtain the nine attributes that make up the Fruit of the Spirit and not produce the fruits that are listed above. These fruits are a natural result of the transformed life.

Now, if you are wondering what this means, or are wondering if you have accomplished all of these three prerequisites, then I believe you have a serious problem. When we do not live holy lives, the Fruit of the Spirit is hidden in our carnality, the works of the flesh, and we cannot exalt Christ! And, yes, a believer can commit these sins if he does not walk in the Spirit. If he does this, he is probably out of fellowship with God. You see, the Christian has two natures, the flesh and the Spirit, and there frequently is a conflict between the two. Every person is tempted when confronted with sin and drawn away with the sins of the flesh. Jesus Christ made us righteous (2 Corinthians 5: 21)—justified. However, we can fall and forget that Jesus originally made us righteous. The Bible says to LOVE one another. If we love one another as Christ loved us we will not commit these sins. Flesh is that sinful element in human natures with its corrupt desires. It remains within the Christian after his conversion and is a deadly enemy to him. Those who practice the deeds of the flesh cannot inherit the kingdom of God (Galatians 5: 21). These must be resisted and put to death in a continual warfare that the believer wages through the Holy Spirit.

I will list these works of the flesh and a brief explanation. Many of these works of the flesh I personally experienced in those involved in the events at Tiny Town Church.

I. Works of the Flesh
1. Adultery (sex outside of marriage)
2. Fornication (sexually unrestrained; any unclean act—spiritual or physical)
3. Uncleanness (Moral or sexual impurity)
4. Lasciviousness (lustful, lewd, wanton behavior)
5. Idolatry (Worship of a physical object or thing, such as power, as a god)
6. Witchcraft (use of power gained from evil spirits)

Attributes needed to eliminate the above Works of the Flesh:

Love: seeking the glory of God

Joy: derived from seeing other Christians advance in the knowledge of the truth

Peace: that tranquility that comes because one is rightly related to God

II. Works of the Flesh

7. Hatred (intense hostility, habitual emotional attitude of distaste coupled with sustained ill will; enmity, opposition)
8. Variance (being in disagreement, discord, dissension or dispute)
9. Emulations (envious rivalry, contention between rivals, jealousy)
10. Wrath (violent anger)
11. Strife (bitter conflict for superiority, cliques or factions; back biting, gossiping)
12. Sedition (rebellion; Incitement or resistance to or insurrection against lawful authority (church or state); divisions.
13. Heresies (an opinion or doctrine contrary to the truth)
14. Envying (painful or resentful awareness of an advantage enjoyed by another, joined with a desire to possess the same advantage; selfish ambitions)

Attributes needed to Eliminate the above Works of the Flesh:

Longsuffering: evenness of character and action that never displays a desire for revenge; patience

Gentleness: beneficent thoughts

Goodness: kind actions

Faithfulness: serving with regularity and buying up all the opportunities with every faculty given to us by God

Meekness: gentlemanliness (applies to both men and women) and in no way includes the concept of weakness.

III. Works of the Flesh
15. Murders (to kill unlawfully with predetermined malice; hatred in the heart is considered murder (John 8: 44; 1 John 3: 15)
16. Drunkenness (Habitual excessive use of alcohol; intoxication)
17. Raveling (wild party or celebration: wild without regulation or control)

Attributes needed to eliminate the above Works of the Flesh:

Temperance: Self-control; it is the discipline of the whole life, including and especially the areas of morality[32]

The person in the flesh is constantly trying to achieve credit, approval, esteem, recognition and praise from God all by his own energy and effort. Therefore he ridicules, mocks, and persecutes the believer. The person in the flesh has to accept human weakness and inadequacies. He refuses to accept that his flesh is corrupt.

Study the works of the flesh above and the attributes that will eliminate that group of works. Then review the previous chapters. I am convinced that the characters in this book, the participants in the Trouble at Tiny Town could not possibly contain the Fruit of the Spirit. It is not possible to participate in such acts and be filled with the Holy Spirit! As I have said before, trouble in the church is the result of either lost souls or loss of filling. It would have been impossible to have these problems if all of the people

---

[32] Ryrie, Charles C. ***The Holy Spirit; 1994.*** Moody Publishers: Chicago

involved had been saved, Baptized in the Holy Spirit, and filled with His Spirit. You cannot yield from the ways of the world and the world's agenda to the Holy Spirit and behave as the characters in this book have done. The action of the Holy Spirit in their lives would not allow that to happen. Each person would have acted differently; Christ-like, considerate, holy and just. The outcome would have been drastically different.

I heard a story about a young man who dives for exotic fish for aquariums He said that one of the most popular aquarium fish is the shark. He said that if you catch a small shark and confine it, it will stay a size proportionate to the aquarium. Sharks can be six inches long and be fully mature. But if you turn them loose into a large body of water like the ocean, they grow to their normal length of eight feet. This also happens to some Christians. I have seen some of the cutest little six inch Christians swim around in a little puddle. But if you put them in a larger arena, and into the whole of creation, only then can they become great! Where are you swimming?

A person without the Holy Spirit has no light and swims around in a little puddle. The light that shines within the individual is made possible by the Holy Spirit. The beauty of holiness can only be seen by the world in the Fruit of the Spirit. When we do not live holy lives, the Fruit of the Spirit is hidden in our carnality and we cannot exalt Christ! Why do believers fail to bear the fruit they ought to bear? Many believers fail to bear the fruit they ought to bear because they are not yielded to God, they are not in agreement with God, and they are not walking in the Spirit! We *must* walk in the Spirit (Galatians 5: 16-17).

We must have victory over the flesh. In order to do this, we must yield to the Spirit. We must yield to the Spirit in these ways:

- Remember Christ's work at Calvary: *Hebrews 12:3; Philippians 2: 4-13*
- Recon yourself crucified with Christ: *Romans 6: 1-11*
- Rest in the Lord by Faith: *Psalms 37:7; Hebrews 4:9*
- Request His will: *Romans 12:2; Ephesians 5:17; 1 John 5::14*
- Receive His work in your life: *Philippians 1:6*
- Rejoice in the Lord: *Philippians 4:4*
- Resist the devil and he will flee: *James 4:7*

Yes, the Holy Spirit bears fruit in those who walk in the Spirit![33]

If you are filled with the Holy Spirit, you will experience an outward expression of praise through speaking in psalms and hymns and spiritual songs; you will experience an inner expression of praise by singing and making melody in your heart to the Lord; you will have a thankful heart; and, you will have the assurance that the Holy Spirit will strive to develop within you a meek and quiet spirit in submission to authority and to other believers (Hebrews 13:17; Ephesians 5:21; 1 Peter 3:4). Being controlled by the Spirit should be the goal of every believer and leads to true submission, harmony in every relationship, and a meek and quiet spirit!

---

[33] Information learned from lectures and discussions: Master of Arts, Christian Leadership and Master of Divinity degrees; and Doctor of Ministry, Pastoral Leadership degree; *The Doctrine of the Holy Spirit*

As you push against the heavy loads of life, have you asked the Holy Spirit to assist you? As you wade through deep grief, have you asked the Holy Spirit to comfort you? As you try to make difficult decisions, have you asked the Holy Spirit to counsel you? As you seek your way along the road of life, have you asked the Holy Spirit to guide you? He is beside each one of us each step we take and He is there to guide us into eternal life with Him.

Here is a story that speaks to this thought. It seems that two pastors were discussing the safety of the children of God as it relates to God always being with us. One says: "Children of God are safe as long as they stay in the lifeboat. He may jump out and if he jumps out, he is lost." To this the other says: "You remind me of an incident in my own life. I took my little son out with me in a boat. I realized, as he did not, the possibility of his jumping or falling into the water, so I sat with him and all the time I held him fast, so he could never fall out or jump out of the boat." But the other guy said, "Yes, but he could have wiggled out of his jacket and fallen out in spite of you". "Oh", said the other, "you misunderstood what I said. You supposed that I was holding his coat. No, I was holding HIM!!" Your heavenly father is holding you tightly, and he has a grip on your life, not just your hand. Once you have placed your faith in Him, you can be sure that you have eternal life![34]

---

[34] Information learned from lectures and discussions: Master of Arts, Christian Leadership and Master of Divinity degrees; and Doctor of Ministry, Pastoral Leadership degree; *1 John-Jude*

12

Walking in the Light

"This is the message we have heard from him and declare to you: God is light; in him there is no darkness at all. If we claim to have fellowship with him yet walk in the darkness, we lie and do not live by the truth. But if we walk in the light, as he is in the light, we have fellowship with one another, and the blood of Jesus, his Son, purifies us from all sin" (1 John 1: 5-7, NIV).

If a person says that he is saved but then lives in the darkness of this world, he is lying. The Bible is straight forward in confirming this statement. A person can be saved and walk in the darkness of sin habitually; but if he does, he will lose his fellowship with God. And, a person who habitually practices sin will put his salvation into question by others! Some will wonder if he was ever saved in the first place. A Christian who walks in the darkness is out of fellowship with God and must ask God for forgiveness in order to regain that fellowship with Him. You see, light and darkness cannot fellowship together. Darkness is the one who is lost.

Here is a story I would like to share with you about one of the members at Tiny Town Church. She is one of the "Seven". Jodie had a strong personality and lots of charisma. Her image was very important to her. She loved attention, being in charge, and the applause of people. She would feed her ego by taking charge of events and travel with those who were superior to her in order to become one of them. She went to church and in public, she talked like a Christian; but in reality, Jodie led a double life, doing whatever she felt she needed to do to maintain control of the church. In her personal life, she was a bully, threatening people with get even tactics in order to control the situation. She walked in the darkness of sin. She had a long list of court cases, law suits and legal proceedings. Her family was out of control too. When it came to her Christian life, Jodie talked the talk but she didn't walk the walk. It didn't take long until her attitude and reputation became known to the entire church family. The new pastor took her aside and told her that while we appreciated all she had done, it was time to let others have the opportunity to serve; one area of service that she needed to share with someone else was that of lay delegate to annual conference. With that, Jodie exploded in a rage and threatened the pastor stating that she would get even with her and the church!

The pastor and the church had seen past Jodie's energetic and do-good personality and into her darker inner self. The light of God's Spirit had exposed Jodie's true intensions. She made it very clear that she would get even. She began dismantling the programs of the church one by one: She took all of the youth to a larger church for their youth program; she convinced these youth to join that church; she called the moms of the Cub Scouts and convinced them to take their boys to that same church and put them in that church's scout program; she called the moms of the after school mentoring program and convinced them to remove their kids from the church's program. She even arranged church bus transportation of those kids to the other church. She began harassing the pastor with disturbing phone calls during the night as well as stalking the pastor by following her and by sitting in a car parked outside the parsonage across the street. During all of this, a snake was found in the fellowship hall kitchen, break-ins to the pastor's office were happening at intervals, and doors that were left locked were found unlocked and open throughout the church. She emptied the packed closet in the youth room of gift items belonging to the church and attempted to change the locks on the closet door hoping this would go un-noticed. When she couldn't get the locks changed, she attempted to change the door knobs and left the old ones and the un-used locks in a box on the floor inside the closet. When she was caught with the items at her home she said that she was selling them in a yard sale for the youth. When she was asked to either return all of the gifts or the money she received for the ones she sold, she returned about one third of the gifts and no money. It was later found out that she was directly or indirectly (depends on how you want to look at it!) involved in the theft of the pastor's covered utility trailer from the church yard. The light of God's Spirit had exposed her true intensions!

People like Jodie declare that because they do good things, attend church or put money in the offering plate, that God would never reject them—that they are acceptable to God. This is not the truth. The Scripture says that no matter how many good works we do, we are not doing the truth if we walk in the darkness. If a person says that they are saved and then lives in the darkness of this world, then they are lying.

A person cannot fellowship with God and walk in darkness. They may be saved, but they absolutely cannot fellowship with God and walk in the darkness of sin. The truth is that man must walk in the light if he is to have fellowship with God. It is impossible to walk in light and darkness at the same time!

Long, long ago, a story was told about a proud fishing pond and a fish. Across the land, fishermen would come and exclaim how clear the water was in this pond. Upon hearing yet another positive accolade, the ponds level of pride began to reach flood stage. "I must be the best and clearest pond in the world", the pond said. It didn't take long for the old fish in the bottom to grow weary of this overdone pride. He had heard it for years and he, the fish, knew better than anyone what was really in this pond. Resting on the bottom of the pond, the old fish began to rapidly flutter his fins. As he did, the motion of the water began to stir up the silt on the bottom. It did not take long for the pond to fill up with a murky cloud. "Stop, what are you doing to me? What have you done? How dare you dirty me up," screamed the offended pond. The fish responded in measuredly distracting words; "I haven't done a thing to you but to show what's been in you all the time".

So I ask you, what is in you? A person who does not walk in the Spirit is full of cloudy, murky, disgusting silt. A person who walks in the Spirit is clear and bright and has the love of Jesus shining out for the world to see. This story shows us the sin that has settled in the bottom of our hearts! Some feel that if they do just enough to stay in tune with God that is enough. They live as they please, eating, drinking and partying as they wish, thinking that it matters little now how they live, just so they believe in God and worship occasionally and do a good deed here and there. Each person gives attention to the Spiritual only as he wishes: only as much as necessary to keep his spirit in touch with God. But his concentration is the body and its pleasure.

There are millions (and have been since Christ) who believe that they are safe and acceptable to God as long as they are baptized, belong to a church, practice the rituals of the church and worship here and there. If they do this, they think that they can pretty much live like they want to during the week. What I know is that God will let you do anything you want to do, but you will have to pay the price for it. Everything we do is important to our Spiritual welfare. Always remember that a child of God does not seek the works of the flesh!

13

Abiding in Christ
The Ministry of Presence

"Do not conform any longer to the pattern of this world, but be transformed by the renewing of your mind. Then you will be able to test and approve what God's will is—his good, pleasing, and perfect will" (Romans 12:2, NIV).

Does the Gospel abide in you? If not, you do not know God! This is a powerful statement. Is the Gospel story being lived out in our lives? Are we letting Jesus Christ live out his life in us? Does the Gospel message abide in you or does it come and go according to the circumstances? (Galatians 2:20).

In order to abide in Christ, there can be no compromise with the Bible. If we live a worldly life our salvation can be questioned. When we accept God in our lives we immediately have eternal life. So, do we abide in Christ? The purpose of abiding in Christ and knowing that we do is so that we can have confidence and not be ashamed at Christ's return (1 John 2: 28-29). What is the proof? The proof of abiding in Christ is living a righteous life, knowing that Christ is righteous and being born again. If we abide in Christ, live a righteous life, know that Christ is righteous and we are born again, then we must be a good match with Christ: we must walk with Him and must abide in Him (Amos 3:3).

Abide: to dwell—to remain fixed; being permanent; continue on and reside in Him; be settled with Him (1 John 2: 28). A person who abides in Christ must live a righteous life with God and man. Since God is love, the person who abides in Christ walks and fellowships with Christ and in love with his fellowman. He walks hour by hour in confession with God and confesses all of his sins as they happen and continues in the Word of Christ and knows the truth!

The person who abides in Christ lets the word of Christ abide in his life. They experience the indwelling presence and witness of the Spirit. They have the power to live like they should (John 15:7). They dwell in love, unity and fellowship with all other believers (John 17: 21-23): Jesus says they all may be one!

The person who abides in Christ bears fruit and lives a very fruitful life (John 15:5). A very important part of abiding in Christ is the fruit you produce. Look around you—what are your fruits?? God expects every believer to live for Him wherever he/she is placed in life, regardless of the circumstances.

The person who abides in Christ loves others and lives and walks in love with others (1 John 4: 12-13). They do not walk in continuous habitual sin (1 John 3:6). They possess confidence and un-ashame-ness in life that prepares them for eternity (1 John 2: 28). They actively surrender themselves to obey God's commandments (1 John 3: 23-24).

The person who abides in Christ loves his/her brother (1 John 2:10). They do the will of God which is that you be saved and abide forever (1 John 2: 17). They experience the continuous presence and anointing of the Holy Spirit (1 John 2: 27). Can you live "in the world" and abide in Christ at the same time? If so, how can it be done? Jesus Christ is coming again—He is coming to judge every man and every woman who ever lived upon this earth (Matt. 16: 27). So, how can we be prepared? We can be prepared by abiding in Christ!!! It will not be easy to do, but the reward is well worth the price the believer will have to pay in order to achieve it.

When Christ died for us, he had our sins on his flesh which was nailed to the tree. He gave his righteous soul to God for us for our sins (Isaiah 53:3). He paid our debt. A person who abides in Christ understands this and lives a righteous life. A person who lives a righteous life knows God and has the nature of God (John 3:3).

Can you tell that I love stories? After all, the Bible is full of them. I love stories, and I would like to share another one with you here: A young boy was trying to move a very heavy box all by himself. He strained and strained and tried several times to move this box. He just couldn't budge the box one inch. Soon, his father came in to the room and asked: "Son, are you having trouble moving that box?" The boy looked up at his father and said: "I have tried everything I know to do but I still can't move it. I am out of strength and out of ideas." The father looked down at his son and said: "My son, you have forgotten one thing that could help you move this heavy box. You have forgotten about me!"

The only way we as believers can live a righteous life is with the help of our heavenly father! These are very difficult times we are living in and it is not easy to always live the way we are supposed to live. Personally, I have had to do a lot of changing in my life in order to establish a lifestyle that is pleasing to God. No one who is born of God continues to sin, practices sin, or keeps on sinning. John emphasizes that one truly born of God cannot make sin his way of life because the life of God cannot exist in one who practices sin (1 John 1:5-7; 2:3-11, 15-17, 24-29; 3: 6-24; 4: 7-8, 20).

The new birth produces spiritual life resulting in an ever-present relationship with God. For one to have God's life in him and to go on sinning is a spiritual impossibility. A believer may occasionally lapse from God's high standard, but he will not continue in sin (1 John 1: 6-10). That which keeps the faithful from sinning is God's seed in him. The seed is God's very life, Spirit, and nature dwelling within the believer (1 John 5: 11-12; John 15:4; 2 Peter 1:4). By faith, (1 John 5:4) the indwelling Christ, the power of the Holy Spirit and the written Word, all believers can live moment by moment free from offense and sin against God.

The believer must break the power of sin in their life by understanding and then applying these five important points to their life. These are:

1. Man is sinful; he needs to be delivered
2. Christ has provided a way for this deliverance.
3. There's a proof of deliverance in Jesus Christ.
4. We have the great conquest of Christ in our deliverance.
5. We are being freed from living in sin as a result of our deliverance!

The believer cannot remain a child of God without a sincere desire and victorious endeavor to please him and to avoid evil (1 John 1: 5-7). This is accomplished only through the grace given to the believer by Christ (1 John 2:3-11, 15-17, 24-29; 3:6-24) through a sustained relationship with Christ and through a dependence on the Holy Spirit. Those who do live in immorality and follow the world's ways whatever they profess, demonstrate that they are still un-regenerated and children of Satan (1 John 3: 6-10).

Just as one can be born of the Holy Spirit by receiving the life of God, he can also extinguish that life by ungodly choices and unrighteous living, and hence, die spiritually. Scripture affirms, "...if you live according to the sinful nature, you will die..." (Romans 8: 13). Sin and the refusal to follow the Holy Spirit extinguish the life of God in the soul of the believer and causes spiritual death and exclusion from the kingdom of God (Matt 12: 31-32; 1 John 5:16).

Our membership in God's family remains conditional on our faith in Christ throughout our earthly existence, demonstrated by a life of sincere obedience and love (Romans 8: 12-14). The rules of behavior have been changed from a life of purity and godliness to a life of self-gratification. A carnal minded Christian winks at sin and justifies his sin with "this is who I am so do not judge me" (1 Corinthians 3:3). God does not wink at sin: He hates it! Carnal Christians live in sin and are not in fellowship with God.

What secrets were the characters in this story hiding? These hidden agendas went against the rules for the church we all pledged to serve. These hidden acts of unrighteousness equaled sin. All unrighteousness is sin. No matter how small or how acceptable we think the unrighteousness is, it is still sin. We doom ourselves if we continue to sin. The point is this: we must strive to live free of sin! The way we live free of sin is to:

- Know that all unrighteousness is sin. There is not an act of unrighteousness that is not sin (Romans 1:18). We must repent and forsake all sin and clearly understand that all unrighteous acts are sin. These acts separate us from God. However, when we repent and believe in Christ and become free of sin, God causes us to be born again and become a new creature in Christ. Now, these are not just idle words. We must think before each word we speak, and each action we take: is this of Christ?
- We must not love the things and systems of the world more than you love God. The world is in opposition to God and we must, therefore, separate ourselves from this world and live for God (John 15:19); for we are born of God. We must strive to create this presence of God in our lives, in our families, and in our communities[35]. We must strive to create a ministry of presence; of being Christ to those we meet each day.

So what is a Ministry of Presence? In this land of plenty and the attitude of *more*, the concept of a ministry of presence is confusing, I am sure. The ministry of presence is the ministry of being…of being Christ…of showing Christlikeness in the way we live, the

---

[35] Information learned from lectures and discussions: Master of Arts, Christian Leadership and Master of Divinity degrees; and Doctor of Ministry, Pastoral Leadership degree; *1 John-Jude*

way we love, and the way we worship our Lord. Who comes to your mind when you think of this definition? Maybe a Priest in his robes or vestments? Maybe a Nun or a Monk? Perhaps the Amish in their buggies? There are groups throughout our world who are different and who, within themselves, have established their ministry of presence. By this presence, we recognize that they are different. Sometimes this difference can be our touchstone to God or Godly living.

We have become critical and judgmental of those around us who are different from *us—the masses*. So, in this chapter, I will explore the Ministry of Presence in my life and the impact this calling has had in my ministry.

Today in the twenty-first century, we expect everyone to dress and act somewhat "normal" or similar, as if that is normal. We tend to have little patience and understanding for those who are different. Many times, people who dress differently and those who have different beliefs are often pre-judged, misunderstood, and the brunt of misperceptions. The understanding that these folks could possibly be on a much deeper spiritual journey than us, and that they, at least, have responded to God's calling, is hard to accept. As a result, we call them "weird", we think them "strange", and we judge them accordingly.

As I journeyed through seminary and ministry, I found myself growing into a much deeper relationship with our Lord. God continued to speak to me and made me more clearly understand that when He called me into ministry, He called me out of the world to be His representative here on earth. Gradually and over a period of time, I began changing my thoughts about the way I looked, the way I dressed, the way I lived, and the way I ministered to others. After leaving Tiny Town and settling into our new culture, I found myself gravitating toward plain dress, dark colors, a covered head, and little or no make-up and not really understanding fully why. At the same time, I gained a new respect for my Amish neighbors and their commitment to their calling to be Amish…to be different…not to conform to this prideful world.

Since my very first introduction to the "plain people", I have had an unexplainable attraction to them. Was it the horses and buggies in the time of fast cars? The plain clothes in a fashion-conscious society? Or, could it be much deeper than that? Could it be that I was especially attracted to their entire life-style as I struggled to follow Christ in my own life, and how they seem to BE their religion, not just practice it for an hour on Sunday?

My fascination for the "plain people" has continued throughout the years and has motivated me to continue to study their religion, their life-style, and their philosophy; and, through this intense study, I have found myself easing into many of their ways and philosophies.

As we entered and began moving through this 21st century, my husband and I began to experience an environmental conversion and an ever deepening Spiritual one. We began to realize that we had to downsize our lives and develop a humility that made us ever grateful for all of our blessings. In areas where we were especially blessed, we shared with others. Fruitless spending stopped; and, *sustainable* became our new norm. We are on a quest for the simple and sustainable life—one built around the core principles of the Amish, extremely similar to first century Christian life.

We have made a conscious effort to unplug from the norm of "more is better" and move into a new way of life that "less is more". That is the basic principle of Amish simplicity. Our biggest project in this respect is the building of our own home. Other Amish principles we embrace—and there are so many more—are concerning finances, simplicity and faith. Amish save more and spend less. We wear out before we replace or purchase which adds to our savings. I make all of my clothes which are a very simple and plain style. I dress modestly which, if in a dress, is long and mostly dark colors and the pattern is a jumper style with a blouse, clergy shirt or t-shirt underneath. In addition, I am committed to wearing out what I already have hanging.

The Amish wear plain clothes that are homemade and simple and include a black apron. Very few wear pattern fabrics although some do. I have some patterned fabrics which are modest. The fashion industry to the Amish is seen as not only a waste but a distraction from the family, friends and their faith…everything that really matters! They avoid using appearance as a form of self-expression or to attract attention to their bodies, which could lead to pride! As I grow in faith, I am striving to be humble and to avoid prideful things. All of these things are things of the world and distract from what is truly important—living a holy life that is pleasing to God in every way; and being a beacon of light to others.

For the Amish, faith is at the center of every thought, every decision, and every action each and every day. They express their faith through example—they model their faith in all aspects of life. If we "English" practiced these same principles in our own lives, our communities would be a much better place to live. So, it is on these principles, based scripturally on first century Christianity that I stand firm. And for me, it came with a cost.

Before moving to Tiny Town, my husband and I went there for a visit with the out-going pastor, Pastor Kim, and a meeting with the Pastor-Parish Relations Committee and a brief meeting with Jodie. First impressions certainly were discouraging. Pastor Kim was dressed in flip-flops, tight knee length pants, a tight blouse with a plunging neckline that revealed a set of grandmotherly bosoms, and a neck and both arms adorned with streams of brightly colored jewelry. If I had been a stranger searching for someone to help me find the Lord, I would certainly not have summoned her. So, confirmation came to me that day that God speaks to others through us; that through our witness, openly and many times without even saying a word, we can lead others into a relationship with Christ.

At Tiny Town, a place where evil was all around, even in the church: being, acting, living, and looking different—not fitting in and not blending in—caused these six church members and leadership and the clergy leadership to be uneasy and uncomfortable in my presence as if someone was hiding a huge secret, and the cost to me at Tiny Town was my ministry there. I found out later that the price I paid at Tiny Town was paid to the devil. Because I lived for Christ and His Church and I never gave in to the "norm" there, I was rescued and given a new life and a new ministry.

The point to this story is this. We are called by God to lifelong learning for His glorification! We should model our lives after the pattern set by Christ. He is our highest example. It is not so much "doing" as "being" a living, healing presence. Each of us are to *be* Christ to every person we meet. We are to live holy lives that are pleasing to God in every way. We are to love our brothers and sisters. Sometimes this will come at a cost. But, believe me; it is well worth it no matter what it is!

14

God's Time
A New Beginning

"I waited patiently for the Lord; he turned to me and heard my cry. He lifted me out of the slimy pit, out of the mud and mire; he set my feet on a rock and gave me a firm place to stand. He put a new song in my mouth, a hymn of praise to our God. Many will see and fear and put their trust in the Lord" (Psalm 40: 1-3, NIV).

Here is the way this story ends. Remember Larry, my pastor and my mentor when I entered the ministry? As I close the pages on this story, I learned that Larry accepted a plea deal on his felony charges and is now serving his time. Most of the Jesus Followers at Tiny Town Church have moved on. The local church's feelings have been ignored. The church is considered by many to be dysfunctional because of the personal agendas and misdeeds of nine people. The church is struggling to stay alive. Alyce remains in a position of leadership in spite of his malicious acts aimed at destroying the people of God and the ministry of one of his pastors. Sadness, strife, and ill-health and even death have fallen upon many of those who participated in the demise of the ministry of Tiny Town Church. My ministry in that state ended and my family and I left devastated and struggling to find a reason to believe that our Lord had not forsaken us.

However, God has taken this sad chain of events and has blessed us all with understanding and clarity. He has made clear to me that it is His will that we follow His laws as written in the Scripture. It is also His will that we follow the laws of our land and our community. If our community happens to be an organized church or denomination, then we are to follow those rules. We are to be in obedience to God's will at all times. We must be yielded to God. When we fail to yield to God, we sin. If we persist in sin and are not yielded totally to God, and used of God, we grieve the Spirit. Ephesians 4:30 says *"Grieve not the Holy Spirit of God"!* God is grieved by every unkind word, deed, thought, impure and uncharitable act, every untrue statement made, and every bitter and un-Christ-like word or deed we say and do.

But, loss is how we come to surrender our lives; that losing really does help us find our way again. I wanted to lead a congregation. I wanted to guide my flock, to help shape their vision, to serve them and to make a difference in their lives. I knew I was called to do this: to spend the rest of my life as close to God as I could get. I really believed, and still do, that pastoral ministry was where I would be able to do just that. As I was preparing to go and serve where I believed God was calling me to go and serve, I had no idea that I would be entering my "desert" filled with pain and suffering. But, that's what it was; and sometimes God does call us into battle, unaware that through the pain and suffering we encounter, we discover God's purpose for our lives after all!

We left Tiny Town Church a broken family; broken in the sense that I did not understand what had happened and we all felt that our church and God had forsaken us; saddened by the sudden end to a ministry filled with hope and grace in a church that was broken when we arrived. We were saddened to leave all of our friends we had made in such a short period of time and saddened for the church family which was now shattered into pieces. The church was left without a pastor and attendance and finances began to plummet to rock bottom.

My mother and brother, who lived with us, seemed to rally around fairly quickly and adjusted to the move to the farm better than my husband and I. I was thankful for that. My husband buried himself in building the house that was an ongoing project and I grieved. I went through all of the emotions of loss and grief and spent about four months feeling sorry for myself until something amazing began to happen within me.

Do you remember the movie, *Field of Dreams?* This movie is fairly old, but still one of my favorites. It is about this guy (Kevin Costner) who has this message placed on his heart to build a ball field in his corn field. He keeps getting messages in dreams, when he is sitting on his porch, and driving in the car. He can't seem to get away from these messages. At one point he thinks he is going crazy and imagining things. He finally realizes that his dreams are heavenly messages being sent to him so the heavenly angels, who incidentally were baseball players before their deaths, would have a place to gather and play ball again.

The message of the movie, on a much deeper level is to listen to God when He speaks to us. So many times we fail to do what God wants us to do—we don't listen to his call upon our lives until after we struggle some. Noah listened and built an ark. Kevin Costner finally listened and built a ball field. I am sure we have all had experiences like this in our own lives.

Several years ago, I had this similar experience. God called us to Community Missions, ministry to family and friends in our new community. Our area is extremely rural. Other than the Amish families all around us, most of the community is unchurched, and there are few spiritual meeting houses in our area. Until recently, we were here only limited amounts of time; but still, the call for our ministry of presence kept coming.

When I look back over the time at Tiny Town Church and how things kept going from bad to worse, God began speaking to me through that situation and telling me that I needed to move. It just was not where God wanted me to be. Sometimes we think that God has called us to do something but that call can be made cloudy by our free will. I have a passion for ministry but in my passion I failed to see clearly where God wanted me to serve. Oh, I could have stayed there in Small Town America and applied for reinstatement and appointment. I could have done a lot of things differently; but, I realized that all of this time, God was calling me back to the mountains, to that beautiful rural farmland and to community missions. I could not hear or heed this call because of the evil hoop-la-la that I was enmeshed in at Tiny Town Church. So, I followed God's call, even though it was difficult, and we journeyed on to our new land.

After arriving there, I began to settle down and think clearly. God's call upon my life became very clear. I began the process of transferring my ministry credentials and we became active in a local church. In addition, the call to community missions rang loud within both of us and we applied for and obtained a charter for our new ministry setting, our little prairie church. This is a place where our family and our unchurched community can gather for prayer and praise. We are small but growing and those who worship with us each week, come with open hearts in joyful praise.

All of our items of worship inside the church have been donated from previous ministry appointments, friends and family and we are so thankful to have each item bring that part of special friends and memories into this ministry experience. God is truly blessing this ministry.

God calls us to make a difference in the lives of others. We are called to reach out and offer the right hand of Christian Fellowship to each soul we meet. We are called to live our faith each minute of our day…to live in communion with God's creation…to have a true Ministry of Presence in our communities and in the lives of our family and friends. We are called to move through this life according to God's time, not ours!

God's time is the right time in all things! God will always do the right things at the right times. God sent His son at the right time. Sometimes we wonder when God is going to do this or that in our lives but we should understand that God does his work at just the right time. It took me a long time to fully realize this: It will always be in God's time. God sent his son into the world at the right time. He was right on time, and he was just in time!

Read Galatians 4:4 concerning God's time. In verses 4-7 we read that there was the fullness of time when God delivered the world: When everything was ready for the world to come of age and to have an adult knowledge of God. If we seek to live for God in all we do: if we truly seek to walk in the Spirit, we will move at God's time and not one minute before.

I love this story that speaks to this very thing: the school's talent show was filled with young children who were more than willing to dazzle the proud parents in the audience. Of all the talent on display that night, one first grader had the most unique talent. Standing on the stage, holding his accordion, he played one note. A few seconds later, he played the same note again. For his big finish, he played that same note a third time. With his shoulders erect and his head held high, he stated to his audience that he had written that song "all by myself!"

Like this little boy, there are many Christians who get stuck on one note and then brag about how wonderful they're doing. But it takes more than one note to make up a song. And it takes more than your best efforts to become free from your fallen nature. It took Jesus Christ, the New Song, and His work on the Cross of Calvary to release believers from the bondage of sin so that we can move through life and into eternity in God's time and with Him.

Are you stuck on one note? Or has Christ freed you and added Spiritual harmony to your life and church? Are you moving at God's time?

Each one of us needs to take a closer look at our lives and ask ourselves my favorite question: *Can the world see Jesus in me?* Can the world see Jesus in the way you treat others? Can the world see Jesus in the way you live your life minute by minute? Can the world see Jesus in the way we care for His creation, which is humanity's highest calling? If you wonder if the answer is yes or not, then you may need to make some adjustments to the way you are living. You may need to build your *Field of Dreams*...to open up your life to the community in which you live...to reach out and share the blessings God has so freely given you. When you live for others then the world WILL see Jesus in you! Had the clergy leadership, lay leadership, congregation and "Satan's Seven" been yielded to the Spirit, I would not be writing this book. The ministry there would have been wonderfully Spirit-filled.

I pray that by sharing my story, others will feel the need for a Spiritual revival in their own lives, churches and throughout their communities. Hopefully, the words I have spoken here will enliven you to walk in the Spirit!

Our New Community

Printed in the United States
By Bookmasters